ABORTION
Women's
RIGHT TO CHOOSE

"I have a woman's mind and a man's might.
No way I'll be silent about women's plight".

—Richard Dexter Russell

"Aristotle believed that humans could learn to be virtuous by making a habit of moral acts—in other words, if you practiced acting like a good person, you would eventually become good. "For the things we have to learn before we can do them, we learn by doing them," he wrote in Nicomachean Ethics, one of his most influential works. "Men become builders by building and lyre players by playing the lyre; so too we become just by doing just acts, temperate by doing temperate acts, brave by doing brave acts".

ABORTION
Women's
RIGHT TO CHOOSE ♀

Here We Stand!

Richard Dexter Russell

Printed in the United States of America
ISBN 978-1-95843-417-8 (sc)
ISBN 978-1-95843-418-5 (e)

Library of Congress Control Number: 2022910327

2022.06.16

MainSpring Books
5901 W. Century Blvd
Suite 750
Los Angeles, CA, US, 90045

www.mainspringbooks.com

If we remain silent, nothing will change!

Am I ready to become a MOM?

1 Corinthians 11:11.

[11]Nevertheless neither is the man without the woman, neither the woman without the man, in the Lord.

Sometimes you have rethink what you have learned,
Why cannot God be a woman?

Water and Woman

Water and woman do not resist they exist.

Water flows. When you plunge your hand into it, all you feel is a caress. Water is not a solid wall; it will not stop you. But water always goes where it wants to go, and nothing in the end can stand against it. Water is patient. Dripping water wears away a stone. Remember that, my child. Remember you are half water. If you can't go through an obstacle, go around it. Water does.

Anger and hate are like flowing water; there's nothing wrong with it as long as you let it flow. Hate is like stagnant water; anger that you denied yourself the freedom to feel, the freedom to flow; water that you gathered in one place and left to forget. Stagnant water becomes dirty, stinky, disease-ridden, poisonous, deadly; that is your hate. On flowing water travels little paper boats; paper boats of forgiveness. Allow yourself to feel anger, allow your waters to flow, along with all the paper boats of forgiveness. Be human.

She loves the serene brutality of the water, loves the electric power she felt with each breath of wet, briny flow. It's is life, I think, to watch the water. A man can learn so many things. Until justice rolls down like water and righteousness like a mighty stream.

This is a lovely portrait inspired by a lovely question asked by my teacher when I was young, which was "what is alive and does not have time and it's everywhere at same time?"

Have you also learned that secret from the river; that there is no such thing as time?" That the river is...

"My book speaks and stands saying, only when open you can come in"?

I honestly love learning and writing about these women and young ladies' stories. I get nauseous and cynical with humanity on how you judge others on their opinion, especially if they are different from yours. Some people have turned away from this subject of Abortion, but I can't. And therefore, their story deserves to be told and retold.

These books are going to split your brain into two more halves. Be prepared to get either pissed off, mind blown, or educated. If you are not capable of reasonable thinking or not believing women have the right to choose. Leave now.

I don't knock anyone having their own beliefs about her body her choice. Even If you don't want to believe women have the right to make decisions about her body. So goodbye and have a happy life. On the other hand, read and deal with my research and my evidence-based interviews.

First, I will give you a history lesson on women history destroying her images and to blame her.

Please don't take my word for it, I promote women and young ladies doing their own research. In order for you to understand Abortion better, you might want to check this first book.

I wrote the book so you can read and pass it on, because I'd received my miracle. Whiten about women and young ladies, in their fight within themselves and others' opinions about their choice. I am passing the book on to you because it's my gift from God to write. And who couldn't use a miracle?

I'm passing this book (as a baton) so you can pass it on to the next person in order to get the race started, to get to the finish line and let everyone know reproductive rights is women's rights.

By now you know you can't win a race looking backwards, so pass the baton forward. Looking ahead and staying the course finishing the race.

As I mentioned beforehand about my authorship, I don't or didn't choose my subject, the subject chooses me. Yes, it probably doesn't make sense to you but it does to me that's how GOD works in us. We don't get to choose what GOD'S gives us, only acceptance is rewarded through GOD'S grace. GODS says His grace is sufficient, and that's good enough for me!

Before you start reading the first book of three, I must warn you will find Grammatical errors and maybe misspelled words. Go ahead and make the changes, in your head or in the book, both belong to you. What it's show's you are reading the book and know I'm not perfect. And it was your choice to buy and read the book. The penitent readers never stop trusting in the power of words.

Also, before you starting reading my book I am not telling or advising anyone to get an abortion or not. I'm a middle-aged black man combat retired veteran and I don't have the right to voice my opinion about women reproductive rights; In my book or any place else. In my opinion, a woman should have every right to choose within her body, her voice, her uterus period!

Many books claim to be life-changers but my book will live up to the promise. Let me give you a head's up about What's going to

Happened to you? you are about to discover or rediscover something about yourself. It will forever change your life. Don't take my word for it, take yours, keep reading!

I spent several years writing these books. I felt writing these books I can write many wrong when it comes to women's rights to choose for her body. I created an outlet that brought me immense delight and opened my mind to new avenues about reproductive healthcare for women and young ladies. Encouraged me to voice my support for the born and unborn. "I felt as though I had begun to live in the midst of the mindset about women and young ladies' right to choose."

What is sadly seared into the common consciousness is the women Rights movements to vote, now it's the Roe V Wade movement women's right to choose. It's my dire hope and prayer that the book makes history by publishing the heartrending voices of women and young ladies, fighting for their rights, that will be reprinted in scores of times.

If we want to continue our phenomenal run as a species, it is essential to understand and embrace women's choice when it comes to reproductive rights. Our evolutionary legacy depends upon it. God gave her birth rights and privileges; it is not your choice to decide for her.

THEY'RE not changing perspective, and not bending or breaking because too much to privileges; will appear as walls but walls knock down become a bridge to provide a pathway forward. My book cannot teach anyone anything in general, only make you think!

Table of Contents

Introduction

"The unprecedented leak of Supreme Court Justice Samuel Alito's draft opinion in a key case striking down Roe v. Wade (1973) has sparked a heated debate, perhaps drawing new attention to the late Justice Ruth Bader Ginsburg's opinion on the key abortion precedent". Please understand the leaker of the draft opinion should not be punished in any way, the person is a hero!

Help me understand something: how is it that a person who doesn't have a UTERUS gets to vote, for the women that have a UTERUS, why are the ones with a UTERUS voting against her's? If Roe V Wade is overturned, around 37 millions women will not have reproductive health care services, let that sink in .If there is no Roe V. Wade Women's won't have rights to choose, It would be pro life only and who is going to take care of the child or children when the mother says no, I didn't want to be impregnated by my rapist's friend or family member or father. I didn't want a baby, because I am 18 years old.

Before you open up the book and start reading, think about your college daughters. Everyone know that young people are likely to have unwanted protective sex therefore leads to pregnancies of young ladies who are in college. Because most campuses in the states don't offer medication abortion in the health care centers, it means the students have to go off campus. And if Roe Vs Wade is overturned there's no place to go. Because abortion health care [isn't] stigmatized, or hard to find but none existence.

I do feel this will be the leading reasons college students drop out of college because not wanting an abortion or can't get an abortion. Because being pregnant and having a child would interrupt their education. inaccessible abortion services the process will interrupting their education. If Roe Vs Wade decision is overturned no clinics aren't open. so it means that students have to take time out of school and drop out of school or walk around campus pregnant.

Picture this first day on campus, an introduction walk around campus just about every young lady you see is pregnant!

They have to skip classes and miss work, because of prenatal appointments. Their extracurricular activities will be their prenatal appointment which may take a whole day to drive or bus all the way down to the clinic. Whereas if you could go to a health care clinic, it's already all set up. You just walk across campus, and be seen, or you go home.

Please keep these statistics in mind, maybe higher not lower.

According to Mr Goggle, Women earn 57% of bachelor's degrees. Among students pursuing a bachelor's degree at a 4-year institution, 63% of women and 57% of men complete their degrees in 6 years. Women are 24.7% more likely to enroll in higher education than men are.
Women are 4.5% more likely to attend private institutions than men are.
44.5% of postsecondary and postgraduate students are men.
55.5% of undergraduate and graduate students are women.

They are not only trying to control the population of races but they are trying to control gender. So I will ask the questions again, what is abortion really all about, you be the judge?

The bequest of the first part of three books is in itself unusual. Indeed, it is heeded that the will of the words are in places to express personal feelings. The best book, or best of any type, is usually regarded as an heirloom to be passed to his readers' major heir. This book is the very epitome of an heirloom, a gift for wakefulness and a touching harsh reality.

While I'm working hard to shine a light on the perilous state of reproductive rights in the United States and women's rights to choose, my work shows how everyone needs to step out and be the vision for the rest of the world.

As my country is threatening to trend backward on abortion rights, the whole world is watching to see how our liberalization will increase abortion access. It's my dire hope my book will play a major role in strengthening the reproductive rights of women and young ladies.

"I needed [Abortion A WOMAN choice, to be more than just scrolling of words on a screen, I need the title to deliver this message (women rights to choose on reproductive health care for her body)? I think abortions and other reproductive health services should be available to everyone for free. I don't want anyone to ever be coerced into parenthood against their will, and I view financial barriers as a type of coercion because you are poor. Conversely, I don't want anyone to feel they "must" choose abortion because they cannot afford the costs associated with pregnancy, childbirth, and parenting. Also, I don't believe Abortion shouldn't be a form of contraception or population control. The decision and choice are and should be between God and woman, and in some cases, her doctor.

American health care should be free, and the parenting parts should be supported by a social safety network strong enough that everyone knows they can live a life of dignity with all their needs covered regardless of what choice they make about parenthood. Abortions, pregnancy-related and childbirth-related healthcare is already free in other countries, that should ideally be the case in America. For instance, Planned Parenthood.

Let's begin: one day, 2007 to 2021; yes, I started writing this book in 2007 and hopefully finished in 2021. Yes, I took some years off, but I always worked hard to gather information about abortion from TV, reading, the internet, and interviewing women and young ladies on abortion. Over the years, I always kept the subject in my mind because I couldn't help thinking about how important it is. I encountered and read several stories and interviews, which led me to write the book.

I've been on the journey to write a non-confrontational book on abortion because the subject is a very controversial and consequential topic. Everyone believes in their hearts and minds they're right, but is there a right or wrong choice when it comes to life? Especially if you are not the bearer of that particular life. But she is.

The subject occurred to me, in 2007. Over the years, I have gathered many bricks to build the book into something I'm hoping is worthy for all women, young ladies, to understand about the born and unborn.

I had the premonition to write the book about abortion using spiritual guidance online, researching many books, interviews, my personal story, and listening to others telling their stories about the born and unborn.

How do I write a very controversial book to please the born and the unborn while not showing any sort of favoritism towards either? God spoke and said there are two sides to every story and the results of the stories rely on their understanding.

In my book I'm trying to get people to understand others' choices and decisions about abortion. But in general, people can behave irrationally, when they believe they are right and this is something many will experience, irrational behavior towards others. In principle, they are passing judgment which is discerning between two individuals.

We need to be able to accept and respect one another through our choices and decisions in order to avoid hardship and chaos. If a person makes the correct choice, you don't do them a favor by criticizing their choice by disrespecting their decisions.

I hope my words will exploded in every direction, simultaneously, in harmony with all receptionists. I'm not looking back, holding back, hesitating on what to say, writing, or even thinking. This book is one of three parts covers a wide array of topics considering abortion, and I hope that you will traverse each books chapter with a sense of change in mind. Think of this as a vessel of hope, a wake-up call, and a reminder of what you ought to do as a child of God.

I'm trying to help decorate the world with a bit of reality with my work because we can be very opinionated about each other today. I try to oblige everyone with the opportunity to realize there are two sides to every story. I am just saying I am a man or color and an author and I don't have the right to make a choice. But I know now we're filled with the purpose to help others, what are you planning on doing about it?

I just write what I feel is right and use the gift given to me. We know that sin destroys our lives, and the pain of leaving sin behind is less than the pain of living in sin.

What I thought and believed was true of humanity. I applied it to my beliefs in every aspect of the book. By the time everything was sorted out, it had become binary and necessary in my sense of understanding. As soon as I realized, like in science, political, religious, moral, and personal convictions could be questioned and might need mending to qualify in writing about the subject. My spiritual belief about abortion should not be quantified by some sort of questioning but could therefore justify my credible reasoning.

But overall, I'm reminded to consult God; I needed to ask how I should write this shocking book. How should I tell people so they can understand? God spoke and said there's two sides to every story: find yours and realize that there are no final definitions, only cross-references. In these middle points, we ought to reach a certain amount of equal respect and recognition.

I remember exactly where I was standing and how it felt when I discovered there was no place to stand, nothing to hold on to but belief and hope, which I know is true. I felt sobered up, yet at the same time, strangely liberated. After all, if there were no absolute answer but the one you can live with, it might be an escape from what often seems to be confining social conformity.

In the past, I was totally in line with supporting pro-life because I didn't feel like I had to try to figure out any other choice because I am a Christian and someone should be the voice for the unborn to speak on my behalf instead. But over the years, I have learned that there are others choices: like Pro-Choice and Women's Right to choose. So, over the years, I continue my research to ensure I get the best possible answer when it comes to a woman's choice because the women need the very best information for clarification on the subject of Abortions.

Preface

First things first: This was a difficult book for me to write. I mean that in *every* sense of the word.

Literally, emotionally, and spiritually: This was a very tangible and literally a moment of silence for need wording written about the subject brought colors red to my very hard and sad eyes but I continue.

A woman is where everything in the cosmos comes to meet, and the cosmos reveals itself through her. Therefore, a woman, to me, is a cathedral where you can take refuge.

This being said, I've published a massive part of my life purpose, in this book titled: Abortion Women rights to choose and any decisions she makes is a powerful Choice. This basically deals with almost every major decision and choice to us, especially to women, and how each of them has structuralist thoughts. I'd highly recommend this as a starting point simply because it's worth it.

Yes, the language might be a bit convoluted at times and maybe a bit disturbing (it is translated from me to you), but why not give it a try and jump into the book if you're interested from the very start anyway?

The first consequence of this is a logical system of meaningful understanding, where you cannot understand anything without knowing the meaning behind it. Especially when it comes to women's struggles and concerns about their bodies, identities, roles, and reproductive rights. Whatever she means or doesn't mean, it is not your decision to make because it is God's choice and the woman's right to decide upon herself. It's inevitably her choice to decide what to do with her body when it comes to abortion.

Hence, to understand 'red,' you need to understand what 'red' isn't: red isn't green, yellow, or a butterfly but are key elements of the makeup of the butterfly. All cultures and society are exactly like language in that it has this very linguistic structure, in that it is a massive logical system of meaning, where you cannot understand anything without understanding the broader context it is a part of. Hence, you cannot understand her without first understanding the woman.

Someone says if you want to hide something, put it in a book and if you want to learn something, start reading it. How do I write this book? Maybe in a film, it foretells a format with which we could talk about external stories and internal stories. Or documentary films that focus on facts, but books focus on feelings, impressions. That's my choice!

I spent a long time ruminating about how I actually feel when writing about women's and young ladies' personal convictions, being pregnant, and how literally writing the book was my only way to convey and uncover it all.

So, I set out to write stories with testimony and interviews and research deeply so that I can write succinctly and accurately. Additionally, I have added pictures taken from the internet and pictures worth a thousand words, which provide a number of cues: body language, facial expressions. The women and young ladies struggle between words as the interviewees struggle to articulate their thoughts because remembering is much harder than forgetting, but they push on.

Everything provides subconscious cues about the many characters. In my book, you can't see any of that, but you can feel their pain. I hope I have described it—all of it; you must choose the moments that I illuminate so as to develop your theme being conveyed.

It was nearly impossible on paper to capture a mother's love while she was considering what to do. I just did not practice enough in that forum. I do think and hopefully am able to convey her compassion, love, courage, and fear, but I tried to do my best even though that might not be enough.

During this part, I aim to answer many unanswered questions: for instance, like What experiences do you hope to take from the book storylines? Is there a lesson to be learned from the book? My biggest challenge was allowing both the born and unborn in their humanity and their ambiguity. I would like to think the book makes readers aware that we all have our differences and qualities, and those ambiguities don't make us less worthy of love, just more human.

It has taken a lot of confidence and courage to write the book, and if anyone knows that, it's you, the reader, and you will learn and know it for its realness and intent of goodwill. I'm also confident with self-love and justice for women and young ladies, reflecting that "you really have to love yourself to get anything done in this world."

Before we begin together on the journey into this section, I would like to ask one question to you, my dear readers, why are people too old to have children or too old to have been involved in getting the woman pregnant, have the right to make a decision on a woman's uterus? Would you mind letting that sink in?

No man has the right to be condescending in the matter of women's it's a shame to grow old without seeing the beauty and strength she's capable of.

Acknowledgements

I tried to imagine the strength and courage of all the women who had or have thought about having an Abortion. Lord knows in most cases; it wasn't an easy decision for her in life. But in some cases, I think abortion should be highly encouraged in certain circumstances (abuse, mental abuse, and intimidation). General infanticide, gender-selective abortion, date-rape drugs, date rape on campus, honor killings, forced marriages, and abuse in lesbian relationships are just some of the many gruesome experiences that women could go through. Moreover, if there are signs of abusive behavior, do not hesitate to seek help. You have to know the general characteristics of abusive partners. It may manifest itself and start with harassment, stalking, and all that stuff, so you have to get a restraining order, flee abusive partners, go to women's shelters, and don't be a part of a murderer's statics, leave the country if you have to!

The greatest problem facing Americans in today's society is the conflict they feel within themselves, so they are angry and unhappy about someone's choice on Abortion because of their religious beliefs or just plain ignorance.

Few are truly peaceful or in harmony because the reason being, they don't believe in anything anymore, neither in themselves nor in the cause and effect of ABORTION. You must believe in something, and if you don't believe in anything, you have failed yourself and lost your sense of purpose in life. Americans have no strong family bonds anymore; brother kills brother, families scatter, and etc.

This is one reason children are so insecure. They don't feel the bonding love of family life. Americans as a majority don't love themselves; therefore, how can they love others?

When you don't love yourself, you can't give love or receive love. Material wealth and power have no place in God's plan for us. Humankind will one day realize who they truly are in the eyes of God, and I pray it's not too late. That truth shall set them free. Human beings will come to understand that they are spiritual beings from the spirit dimension, living a human experience in this physical dimension we call Earth.

I also like to acknowledge why I tell their stories, being a man of faith. Because the power of the sword and the pen isn't greater than the power of women. Also, to let her know she is not alone in her struggles with her choice. It is the story of many girls and women who made the sacrifice one way the other. I think realizing that you're not alone; that you are standing with millions of your sisters around the world is vital.

I like to acknowledge the blank pages in the book as they represented the exciting infinitude of the new age, and a life lived outside the boundaries of conventional reading. I intentionally left two blank pages after each chapter for the reader to take notes about the chapter and create your own journal. This allows the book to become interactive reading.

Chapter 1

Women's Right to Choose

Pro-choice advocates state that the Bible does not address abortion, so the decision should be given among the individuals. When we are given a choice, most of us have something we would change about ourselves. Our aptitude, wealth, or appearance would be a starting point for some. Sometimes it could be the smallest details or parts of ourselves that we deem as a part of us that needs room for improvement, and sometimes, it is those qualities that are innate and very difficult to change. Why do we put ourselves into these narratives and thoughts? I do think that maybe, it's because we have the freedom to think of ourselves and the choices we are bound to make. This should be the same case for women all over the world in that they get to make a stand for themselves, for their bodies, and for what they believe is right.

There are things about ourselves that can be changed and other qualities that we have to learn to live with—all of which were made by God. The same God who created everything in the entire universe also knows how many hairs are on our heads. He is all-knowing and omnipotent, transcendental in the matter of everything in this world. Since he is all those attributes, I am pretty certain that the essence of women is valued by Him. It is only right for us to not only look at ourselves, to look up to God, but also look at our women and how we are treating them as fellow humans, as fellow people.

Psalm 139 reminds us that we were designed by a Creator that took time with every detail that makes up who we are. Our bodies are composed of between 30 and 40 trillion cells—and those cells reproduce themselves every seven years. We have complex and marvelous bodies created by God for our free-will decisions and choices. We are made and crafted in the image and likeness of God. Each and every one of us had been given a chance to follow His footsteps, spread the warmth and promise of His teachings, and become better people in service of Him. There is no doubt that we should live in accordance with His teachings. How do we do this? We respect our women, we give them their rights, and we value the choice that they make for themselves because they are able to and deserve it entirely.

I'm trying to express gratitude for the wonder of creation in my book even though I don't have the medical knowledge. I'm sure children, teens, and even adults struggle with the realization that nothing about them is an accident. We were created intentionally by God. Every aspect of our innate humanity has been made through the guidance of God. We are therefore tasked to take care of ourselves, care for others, and especially care for our women who have long been struggling to face the challenges of this society.

God understands and is sympathetic to our insecurities, even in our decisions and choices. Genesis 1:26-27 says that God made humankind in his "image" and "likeness." When we ask for help, God is willing to comfort us and remind us how much He loves us. In His wisdom and power, God chose to give us life, right now, at this point in history. We now have the surmounting ability to participate in God's control or management of the earth's resources and creatures because through us, He is able to govern our hearts and minds in hopes of peaceful protection of women and people. It is a precious gift! We are given the free will to give warmth and appreciation to all our women, peers, and fellow people. God forgives, and he shows us mercy. That is enough proof that he is a supreme being capable of letting us achieve our greatest goals while also sharing goodness to others, to our women.

It's also because of Adam and Eve, especially Adam. It became a story continuously told wherein others started to believe in blaming women from the notion of what Eve did to tempt Adam. Was this really the truth that we seek? For us to blame each other, to put out the shame to one another for the deeds that we committed? Aren't we supposed to be the shepherds that respect, love, understand, protect, and give warmth to each other? Once upon a time, the belief was most important and ingrained to this patriarchal entirety in society, for some greater morality, but upon further inspection and practice has only hindered the rights of women. There is no denying that this underwhelming action towards women exists. If you ask a woman if she had ever felt unsafe and unprotected at least once or a couple of times in her life, her answer will always amount to a 'yes.' We must not deny these circumstances occurring to our women because tolerating such a thing just tells us that we are no stewards of God. We are enablers of perpetrators and oppressors who disrespect and discriminate against our women.

Every time the Bible (or any other doctrine) doesn't make logical sense, when it comes to women, I suggest you take that for what it is worth and not to heart, trying to manipulate your mind into "fitting it in."

If you want to believe, that's totally fine, but don't be surprised when you're absolutely wrong, since those could become more skeptical to you.

To a certain extent, I cannot help but raise the fact that oftentimes, men have always needed to feel like they have to control what a woman should or should not do with her body. This apparently has divided us even more. I do know that men, for some reason, wish to remain dominant and protect their prideful 'masculinity' by limiting society's construct of women's roles and rights. If they are, even in the smallest aspects and instances, threatened by the aims and actions of women in thriving to protect themselves, can we really trust them with their perceptions of what is right? Is the ego of a man really that fragile, or is it much more important instead of the reproductive and civic rights of all the women across the globe?

What I believe for the first time in his entire life, Adam's conscience was stricken, and, like many of us, he felt compelled to deflect the blame for what he knew should not have been done onto someone else. If you think about what he said, he actually blamed God when he said the woman "you gave me" gave me the fruit. What is so right about passing the blame? What is so good about preserving a man's self-interest if we are inching away from the values, we are supposed to be emanating within ourselves?

Genesis 3:12 NWT — The man said: "The woman whom you gave to be with me, she gave me fruit from the tree." What could we interpret out of this? How did we reach a point where we are continually degrading and belittling women when at the end of the day, they play such a great part in our lives and are capable of so much more?

Being a Christian, my first thought is to love thy neighbor as yourself and judgment belong to God. Therefore, whatever choice women make is her right, and that judgment is between woman and God. Why should men feel like they have to have the most important part out of it? Why does the narrative always have to fit what men are comfortable with? What about women? Are we just going to ignore the constant struggle they are experiencing each and every day? What does that make of us as Christians? What about the other religions? Indeed, our cultures are different, and we may not believe in the same thing at all times. But shouldn't we recognize that above all, women's lives and rights are just as essential as men's? Why should men then have the final say in women's reproductive rights? Towards abortion? There is no linear experience, and it does not conform to only one. How could men ever dare to discredit those women who suffer these consequences under the hands of the same kinds of people? Of the men themselves?

Abortion has been a highly debatable and contested topic in any culture for the past forty years. Proponents on both sides wave statistics and viewpoints that many sincerely believe to be the only right way. This constant division has separated our people and created a wide gap and disparity. It is a necessary battle to earn back the rights of women to choose for themselves.

For the sake of clarity, let's define the terms "pro-choice" and "pro-life." For the purposes of this chapter, "pro-choice" will be defined as "the belief that a woman should have the legal right to abort her unborn child at any point in the pregnancy." Pro-choice advocates and believes that abortion is a personal decision and should not be limited by the government or anyone else. "Pro-life" will be defined as "the belief that every human life is sacred and no one, including the mother, has the right to end an innocent life." Pro-life advocates and holds the view that life from the moment of conception should be protected and never taken away. No one has the power to do such a thing, but the compromise of thousands of women then becomes at stake if this notion is supported.

My third choice is women's rights to choose most definitely on certain extenuating circumstances such as time, causation of the pregnancy. For example, any form of sexual abuse and incessant behavior should be taken into the discussion because a woman has not only gone through trauma but consequences as well. Abortion isn't an acceptable means or form of birth control.

So, should a Christian be pro-choice or pro-life? A Christian, according to the Bible, is someone who has accepted God's offer of forgiveness through Jesus' death and resurrection. Salvation is a gift of God through faith in the finished work of God. With that being said, be your own judge about her choice, don't dare undermine her choice.

To know and understand the love of the creation of women is to know and understand the creator's intention. Women all over the world are the art created by the artist (God). Somewhere all over the world, there is a woman who provides such warmth, strength, and influence. Why should we look down on our women then? In order to love and care for our women, we must follow God's protection and respect of women. We are not the supreme being. We are just people, and so are women. We are all equal in God's eyes, so why should we make women think that they are far below the league of men?

Being a Christian and a man doesn't make me eligible to answer why I feel women are the life of all things. But what I feel gives me eligibility is the fact that all humanity starts with women, including me, and this, therefore, gives me the gifted ability to write about them. I honor them, all the women, and society should do the same.

The most beautiful thing I have encountered besides the mother is the art of child bearings. It is not easy, and the tolerance of pain by mothers is such a heroic move. No one has that much courage except the women who have to go through such a challenge. And yet, women do it with much passion and care, with all their efforts because they are capable of feeling and loving. For me, the most beautiful and wondrous encounter is a baby being born and the laughter of babies. In my research, babies take their first form in the mother's womb. The mother and the father come to know about the feeling of love, something which can't be explained because they can just understand it through feeling it themselves.

Every month after month, a baby goes into transition. Each month comes when a mother feels her baby kicking. The first kick of the baby is something that will bring tears to your eyes. Every woman knows the feeling of the time when it comes to giving birth to her baby. Trust me, guys, we might even feel that we will die during the process, but the women endure it to bring that little happiness out into our life, to complete our life entirely.

It is said that babies coming into the world have to first cry because this is important, not only for them but also for their mothers. It gives their mothers a will to wake up and carry their child, to keep on going and fighting. This gives mothers a massive and gigantic sense of value, responsibility, protection, and love for their children to take care of. Another most wonderful and important analogy is that babies not only take on birth but they also give birth to their mothers. Babies are indeed the most wonderful creation in our life.

(Women love her; she will always bring happiness in our life. :)

The most beautiful thing on earth is our heart's gratitude to the Supreme, to the divinity in humanity, to God. The best and most valuable thing on earth is the ability to create. Women's ability to procreate is unparalleled, and it will remain so throughout Eternity. And many women who went through the process realize they never truly lived; afterward, they only just exist. This just means that women's feelings towards abortion should be taken into account heavily.

The world has been harsh to people, especially to women. I have long been able to see and observe this characteristic of control towards a certain population of the world. Wherever in the world, you look, especially from decades and centuries ago, you can see a vast disparity in how women are treated and viewed. We must never deny this. I write with clear intent, with opened ears, and a longing heart. We have been taught to love, care, and respect one another. And yet, throughout history, we are not acclaimed for fulfilling this duty all the time. We have our fair share of darkness and bad records. There is no use denying this matter because we can never deny or lie about this. We may try to bury it deep in our hearts, but women, for a long span of time, have constantly been fighting for their role, their rights, and even their lives. Abortion? It is such a debated issue. Even if you look at it in a religious or civic aspect, people, even men, have so much to say in the matter. Why is that?

Chapter 2

Abortion through Society's Lens

There is a sense, when you read this part and section where you finally let the words unfold and you see that people could be very black and white on talking about abortion. But if you take the time to look closely, they're not. People have very mixed views on it, but women's right to choose should have overwhelming support throughout it all. The voices of other women remain significant to me, and I wish society would also look at it that way. For centuries, women have been placed at the pedestal of insurmountable perceptions and expectations. In the old and the new, there is always a gender norm to talk about. Even in the eyes of God and in all other religions, the role of women, in society, in their households, and within themselves have been constantly redefined by time and circumstances. Before we have witnessed the rights and the cries of the women of countless generations, so now I wish to emphasize the fact that discussing all about the essence of women in whatever society they belong in is an issue that is bounded by traditional outlooks while being challenged by modern propositions.

This book has been my rooted reason for giving light to recognizing women and their utmost importance to any community. It is through God's eyes that we are guided by the premise that women hold so much space and essence in the world. I refuse to be blinded by the comfort and promises given to women, and yet control is instigated when the right to choose for themselves and their bodies are at stake. This is why I continue to write and fight for the women and the voiceless.

It is with the best regard that I aim to give acknowledgement to all the women around the world. They are the pillar of inspiration, the torch of strength and unrestricted definitions of women, and they are human beings with feelings that contribute to society. They deserve the spotlight for their grit, empathy, and warm hearts. Kudos to you, women from all over the globe. Keep fighting.

Why do men want to control women's uterus?

When you go back to the beginning, to the very first story in Genesis 1, you will remember that God created one human creation and divided it into half: male and female. The entire story begins with equality! Today, thirty centuries after this story was first written down, men and women now stand equally before God. This was an unbelievably hard-earned victory that involved going back and pulling apart the layers of discrimination that were plastered onto this story and the structures underlying the prospects of gender norms in society. Going back to the original story, where we can see equality and giving importance to women, a see-sawing of power, an equilibrium — that's what the story is trying to say to us. It is not separating us apart but making us realize that men and women were both created in the same image and likeness. One was not meant to dominate the other, both needed to cooperate and work well in order to be in harmony with each other. That was the whole point of Genesis and yet, people still seem to forget about that. Most people even go so far as to reject this logic even when it is so clear and explainable already. Blaming others, pinpointing and seeking accountability for things that have happened so many years ago.

When you go back and start looking at it, I'm hoping you realize that they've got the story wrong, the story was weaponized as a way to elevate men and keep down women in whatever pursuit you could picture out. And if we're going to have some meaning from the past and the middle of this conversation, we have to see the story for what it's really saying to us; how much it uncovers our patriarchal tendencies, gender discrimination, and classist attributes that formulate these disrupting instances. The order and the truth reveal to us that both men and women are necessary in building and nurturing the whole of humanity, no one is inferior from the other.

In the traditional interpretation and gaze, equality did not conform to roles and this disparity had created centuries of different treatment towards men and women. This goes to say that our social construct has led us to believe that women are much more limited in nature and have to rely on men. This should not be a case of gender but a turning point of individuality. In equality, there is no full-on dependence that happens with one person towards another person. It should not be treated like a woman cannot live without the guidance and presence of a man. A woman is fully capable of doing a man's work and this proves that even women can be fully capable of reaching up to the standards that men have set up for themselves. What does this mean? It tells us that humans are codependent with each other, it's not just the women but it is also men who need this connection and engagement.

I'm tired of having a parade of men stepping up to the microphone to tell women how to run their bodies. Have any women tried to stop you from getting a vasectomy? So why are you getting into her business? Why do men always have a say? it's not their bodies, why should they be so concerned with it when they are not directly and literally affected by it?

There are those men who think they should be in charge of organizing women's reproductive rights. I'm going to show you some strong reasons why this shouldn't be the case to focus on. Let me make myself perfectly clear. Women know what's best for themselves. I've had enough of men feeling like they have to be the hero and the main character in every narrative that doesn't even concern them and affects them to the point that they cannot function properly. It is such a sad truth in our reality nowadays. Why should we put up with that anyway? Why should women compromise themselves to fit what men desire and want in society?

One thing I have learnt is how gray an area this is for people. I'm hoping to widen the scope of people's opinion and perceptions by discussing this section of the book. By telling people about women's rights to choose what happens to her body is a good start to bring about more issues in the future that we need to raise as well. I've been able to gauge so much of men's so-called opinion but the only thing that matters is hers, the woman's voice because it is her body and it is her temple to talk about in the eyes of God.

The American concept of religious freedom and the controversial push for it in the nation's courts and political arena is equally unnerving and surprising. This occurs in a way how religious freedom and religious revivals fueled competition in the religious marketplace; how movements for social reform—from abortion to human rights have stirred courts and laws alike. It is very ironic how religious faith influences conflicts in America when it comes to reproductive health care cases and rights but then again, we have to look at this from all angles at the same time in order to not discredit any viewpoint that may seem important for analysis.

It is quite evident and apparent that men just kind of want to have control over women's case of life, death and birth. Come on, we can afford to cut men some slack here but a discussion still has to be made. It's always been tough on guys but imagine how tough it is for women. You cannot deny that despite all those adversities, females pull off the ultimate magic trick in the universe: to fight and be heard because they are more than just mothers, sisters, daughters, and child-bearers. They are women with individual pursuits, dreams, and aspirations.

Feminist philosopher Mary O'Brien speculated that patriarchy emerged 8,000 or so years ago as a way for men to control women's reproduction. Isn't it funny because that's a lot of work for men! You know, getting to know who's superior and setting up a whole system of laws, beliefs, social structures, and religions, then forcing men into submission, and then going to war to conquer other groups of women? What a complex kind we have become just because we needed to sort out that triumph men always sought to acquire and boast about.

Women should have the right to control their own bodies and reproduction because she knows and can be trusted to know what's best for herself. How do we know that? Because most women know they should have the right to choose to have an abortion if they wish and, overwhelmingly, they should have the right to safe and effective forms of birth control and reproductive health care. And since I, as a man, say they should have that right. This does not make me any less of a man. In fact, it just proves that masculinity should not be defined in making women feel inferior. Masculinity is supporting women wholeheartedly as well.

With a wave of fresh attacks on women's rights, now is the time for us, as men and women, to speak out with loud and clear voices to express our profound concern for this long-held issue. We urge men: to speak out in your communities, media, places of worship and halls of government in support of a woman's right to safe and effective means of contraception and abortion; to oppose arbitrary laws and regulations that make it difficult to obtain these medical services and thorough assistance and care; to keep abortion out of criminal law and see it solely as a medical procedure to be utilized by a woman in consultation with her doctor; to support enhanced government funding and policies to ensure that women's reproductive rights are not only rights on paper, but that all women, regardless of where they live, where they work, or their financial resources, can obtain safe and effective birth control and abortion if they choose to do so; to support positive sexuality education in our schools that focuses on healthy relationships, sexual decision-making, and reproductive health (including the safe and effective use of birth control); and to fully support political candidates who support these rights.

Society is constantly involved in shaping the lives of various people. When a choice is made, there is this thing that we call a 'chain reaction'. When men continue to propagate that it is normal and okay to deprive women of their rights to choose for what's best for their future and their bodies, it will always be an ingrained problem that people do not overcome. It is through the eyes of the masses that we recognize just how easy it is to make people follow rules, to make them believe that something is acceptable even when it is ethically and morally wrong. No one else will speak if not for the brave ones. There is this term in moral philosophy that we call moral courage. It is the ability and the skill to rise up, to take a stand, and to fight against the dominating norms in order to change what is wrong.

Most people think that since our days have been much more innovative, fast-paced, and rapidly growing changes circulate around us, our women already feel protected and safe. No, they are not. Society still condemns women for trying to take control of their own lives. Society tells them it is wrong to think about your circumstances because your ancestors said so. But wasn't change always a scary thing? Change isn't always bad. You must remember that we are definitely at a different time and generation from those before us. We may have learned a thing or two from them but it doesn't mean that there are progressive actions we can make to counter the backward nature of the mindset from before.

Let us not encourage having more victims of naught and abuse. Women who encounter such horrible treatments are changed forever. If society cannot fathom the gravity of having more cases of distraught and disrespect towards a woman, then we will totally not be able to grow as people of God. We must learn to abide by the changes of time because just like what most people say, change is the only constant thing in this world. No matter how much society wishes to maintain order, beliefs, practices, and traditions that try to hinder the attainment of openness and social consciousness, then the lens of society will always stay small, will always be clouded with prejudice, bias and fear, and growth is now such a far-fetched matter. In order for us, humans, to grapple the wisdom and warmth of God, we must seek that purpose of understanding the world through our own best intentions. If we cannot even do that, how do we create a future generation where women are finally empowered and not dejected and objectified?

It has been far too long now and our women must receive the social justice they deserve. Are we too keen on focusing only on one option? Pro-choice or Pro-life? Why don't we consider pro-women instead? Think of all the unwanted pregnancies every woman faces every day. Most of them undergo and experience such harsh environments. Earth, our world, was a land of promise. It is supposed to be a land filled with God's purpose being accomplished for us. But what have we become? We blame each other, seek chaos among each other, and we think more about our individual satisfaction instead of as a collective body. Yes, it is important to care for oneself. However, is it truly self-care if men, who prod along the roads and can go home at night without worrying about anything because of their gender privileges, keep on taking account of each step made by a woman?

Abortion is not the biggest problem of the world but IT IS A BIG PART OF WOMEN'S LIVES. You cannot dictate a womb to control itself. There are so many of the women's population and yet so few are reported to be treated like equals. It indeed saddens me to hear such a thing, that our perpetrators may not be wholly based on gender but if you look at statistics, most men and a few (highly rare) women commit atrocities to their fellow men and women. Now tell me, are you going to tell a girl who was raped and abused to keep the baby of her molester? Who do you think you are?

What about those children who are forced to come out of this world even if their parents are not prepared? Think of all those suffering families who are forced to have their children work at a very young age because they were not taught openly about taking extra care with their sexual health? Do we even have sexual education in schools and communities in order to teach men and women safe and responsible sex? You cannot deny that this is a natural and humanistic process. You cannot stop every single person here on Earth from doing such a thing, so don't you think it is better to minimize the consequences by focusing on what we can do as members of society? Let us not create a generation where children are not cared for any longer. Let us not force a woman to raise a child when she can barely raise herself (especially in the most unlikely surroundings that cannot foster a healthy childhood and motherhood for a woman and her child).

Chapter 3

The Truth About Abortion

Like an ever-growing number of men around the world, we think women should control their own bodies. I hold these truths as deep moral beliefs. All humans should have the right to autonomy and bodily integrity. For women and men, this often means the same thing. But for women, it has an additional meaning: the ability to make choices regarding whether she will bear a child. Bearing a child is no easy task and it is such a big decision that can alter a woman's life forever. So why should we leave it to the ones with no uterus to speak for this matter when in fact, we should listen to the voices that require us to reflect upon ourselves?

We believe that no man should be able to force a woman to bear a child that she does not want. No man should be able to limit her ability to obtain safe and effective means of contraception because it is not our place to decide for the women.

We believe that the government has many important roles in our society. There are those (including some who support this statement) who believe that abortion and contraception interfere with the workings of God. Men who support women's choice respect each person's right to make their own birth control and abortion choices based on their beliefs. At the same time, we share the belief that none of us has the right to limit or interfere with a woman's moral position or personal choices, nor interfere with health care providers who are assisting her right to exercise those choices. This interference only occurs when a third opinion is needed in urgency and the scale of the concern affects many people and not just the woman herself.

As men with strong moral beliefs, and as men who vies for women's rightful choice to protect, preserve, and defend themselves, we especially emphasize our belief that no man – no husband, no boyfriend, no judge, no doctor, no politician, and no religious leader – should have control over a woman's body. Ever!

Reproductive justice

At this point in time, I'm gearing on talking about reproductive justice in America for all. Utilizing my book platform in the fighting can ensure that people have access or option to pursue abortion, contraception, comprehensive sex education, and prenatal and childbirth care.

Women had no control over most aspects of their lives. Why? Because once they were married, they lived in fear, every single month, that they would become pregnant. It didn't matter if there was insufficient income to feed more children, or insufficient space for them, or if their health and stamina wasn't sufficient for them to take care of the children they already had. Women died at younger ages.

Families lived in poverty. Historically, in most cultures' childbirth was a woman's affair, and there were some methods of aborting unwanted children, which disappeared in the US when physicians had laws enacted making midwifery illegal, in large part to increase their business. These factual happenings were the dark parts of women's history and turning a blind eye to this matter just makes us an enabler and a part of the problem.

Why do most women fear speaking openly about abortion?

Even though abortion is a common experience in the lives of some women, what I read and understand is that it's usually kept as a secret. Women fear being judged, arrested, or mistreated, so the topic is taboo, and they do not share their stories, until now, I have given them a platform to express their experiences. Moreover, I read despite the requirement of professional confidentiality that it is not uncommon for doctors and nurses to report women to the police when they arrive at hospitals seeking emergency care for complications from unsafe abortions.

I hope the stories will always be remembered, as it represents a significant change in the litigation and advocacy strategies that we pursue in Brazil for the decriminalization of abortion and protection of women's lives.

It is time to tell more women's stories and to ensure that abortion is a part of the public and political debates. I know that telling stories is not enough to guarantee rights, but it is certainly a step towards eventually recognizing them and creating policies that will navigate better opportunities and a promising outlook for women.

It's totally normal to have a lot of different emotions after your abortion. Everyone's experience is different, and there's no "right" or "wrong" way to feel. Most people are relieved and they don't regret their decision. Others may feel sadness, guilt, or regret after an abortion. Lots of people have all these feelings at different times. These feelings aren't unique to having an abortion. People feel many different emotions after giving birth, too.

1. Bible forbids abortion

Should it matter what the Bible says about abortion? The United States is not a theocracy. Still, given the certitude of abortion opponents that abortion violates God's Word, it might come as a surprise that neither the Old Testament nor the New Testament mentions abortion—not even one word.

It's not that the Old Testament is reticent about women's bodies, either. Menstruation gets a lot of attention. So do child- birth, infertility, sexual desire, prostitution (death penalty), infidelity (more death penalty), and rape (if the woman is within earshot of others and doesn't cry out . . . death penalty). How can it be that the authors (or Author) set down what should happen to a woman who seeks to help her husband in a fight by grabbing the other man's testicles (her hand should be cut off) but did not feel abortion deserved so much as a word? Given the penalties for nonmarital sex and being a rape victim, it's hard to believe that women never needed desperately to end a pregnancy, and that there was no folk knowledge of how to do so, as there was in other ancient cultures. Midwives would have known how to induce a miscarriage.

If people are fighting and hit a pregnant woman and she gives birth prematurely but there is no serious injury, the offender must be fined whatever the woman's husband demands and the court allows. But if there is serious injury, you are to take life for life . . .

Contemporary abortion opponents interpret this passage as distinguishing between causing a premature birth (fine) versus causing a miscarriage (death penalty), which is indeed what most modern translations suggest. Unfortunately, for abortion opponents, at least one thousand years of rabbinical scholarship say the fine is for causing a miscarriage and the death penalty is for causing the death of the pregnant woman. If anti-abortion exegetes are only now finding in this rather obscure passage evidence for an absolute biblical ban on abortion, you have to wonder why no one read it that way before. The Talmud permits abortion under certain circumstances, in fact requires it if the woman's life is at stake.

The New Testament was a second chance for God to make himself clear about abortion. Jesus had some strong views of marriage and sex—he considered the Jewish divorce laws too lenient, disapproved of stoning adulteresses, and did not shrink from healing a woman who had "an issue" (vaginal bleeding of some sort) that had lasted twelve years and would have made her an outcast among Jews. But he said nothing about abortion. Neither did Saint Paul, or the other New Testament authors, or any of the later authors whose words were interpolated into the original texts.

2. Women are coerced into having abortions

Abortion opponents claim girls and women are frequently forced or bullied into terminating wanted pregnancies. That 64% of women "feel pressured to abort" is a claim that shows up over and over. As the journalist Robin Marty was the first to report, the 64% statistic comes from a 2004 article in Medical Science Monitor, "Induced Abortion and Traumatic Stress: A Preliminary Comparison of American and Russian Women" by Vincent M. Rue, Priscilla K. Coleman, James J. Rue, and David C. Reardon. But David Reardon is a major anti-abortion activist, tireless promoter of "post-abortion syndrome," a condition rejected by the American Psychological Association, and director of the anti-abortion Elliot Institute. (According to its Web site, the name was "picked from a baby names book" because it sounds both friendly and academic.) His PhD in biomedical ethics comes from Pacific Western University, an unaccredited correspondence school. Medical Science Monitor, an online journal, has published other spurious research, for example, papers defending the discredited vaccine-autism connection. In 2012 it was exposed as one of a circle of journals that agreed to inflate their citation rankings by citing one another.

There are a number of problems with the paper in question, which was actually not about coercion but a comparison of post-abortion trauma in American and Russian women. Its sample was tiny (217 Americans), self-selected, far whiter and more middle-class than the general population of women who've had abortions, plus the women were reporting on abortions a decade earlier. Half thought abortion was wrong; only 40 per-cent thought women should have a right to it. Thirty percent said they had "health complications" after the abortion, which could mean anything. (According to the Guttmacher Institute, only .05 percent of first trimester abortions have complications "that might require hospital care.") Interestingly, the American women, though not the Russian women, reported staggering amounts of violence and trauma in their lives before the abortion.

How common is it for a woman to be pushed into an abortion she doesn't want? In a 2005 Guttmacher Institute survey, 1,209 women were asked their reasons for choosing abortion. Fourteen percent cited "husband or partner wants me to have an abortion" and 6 percent cited "parents want me to have an abortion." (Interestingly, both these answers were down from a similar survey in 1987, when 24 percent of women mentioned the wishes of husbands/partners and 8 percent mentioned those of parents.) But when asked to name the single most important reason, less than 0.5 percent each cited the wishes of husband/partner or parents.

3. Abortion is dangerous

Anti-abortion literature is full of stories about women gravely injured or even killed in clinics. Such places exist: A woman died in Kermit Gosnell's Philadelphia clinic, some were injured, and all received inferior care. Steven Brigham has been in legal trouble in several states. Such doctors stay in business because they are cheap, they are in the neighborhood, they perform abortions later than the law allows, and they zero in on low-income patients who, sadly, are used to being treated badly by people in authority. No doubt there are other inferior clinics out there. But only in abortion care do the few bad providers taint all the others—and taint them so much that opponents can pass laws that would virtually shut down the entire field in the name of patient safety.

And yet, abortion is remarkably safe. The CDC reports that from 2003 to 2009, the most recent period for which it has figures, the national mortality rate was .67 deaths per 100,000 abortions. In 2009, a total of eight women died due to abortion. Tragic as that is, compare it with fatal reactions to penicillin, which occur in 1 case per 50–100,000 courses. And what about Viagra? According to the Association of Reproductive Health Professionals, it has a death rate of 5 per 100,000 prescriptions. But you don't find legislators calling for a ban on Viagra.

Really, though, there is only one directly relevant comparison of risk with respect to abortion, and that is pregnancy and childbirth. The death rate for that is 8.8 women per 100,000. Continuing a pregnancy is 12 to 14 times as potentially fatal as ending it. (And the maternal mortality rate is rising in the US even as it is falling around the world.) Curiously, no one suggests that obstetricians be compelled to read pregnant women scripts about the dangers that lie ahead before sending them home for 24 hours to think about whether they wish to proceed.

4. There are too many abortions

Sometimes what people mean when they say there are too many abortions is that we need to help girls and women take charge of their sexuality and have more options in life. According to the Guttmacher

Institute, in 2011 abortion declined by 13 percent from 2008, mostly because of better access to birth control and to longer-acting birth control methods like the IUD. That is very good news.

But often what people mean is that women are too casual about sex and contraception. When Naomi Wolf writes about her friends' it-was-such-good-Chardonnay abortions, she is saying women get pregnant by accident because they are hedonistic and shallow. It is difficult to come down hard on abortion as immoral, to insist that the ideal number of abortions is zero, as Will Saletan maintains, without blaming the individual woman who got herself into a fix and now wants to do a bad thing to get out of it.

5. Abortion is racist

In February 2011, a three-story-high billboard popped up in New York City. Featuring an adorable little black girl in a sweet pink dress, it proclaimed, "The Most Dangerous Place for an African American Is in the Womb." The previous year, billboards in Atlanta showed a little black boy with the slogan "Black Children Are an Endangered Species." The brainchild of Life Always, a Texas anti-abortion group, these signs, and similar ones around the country comparing abortion to slavery, aroused so much indignation from black women that they were quickly taken down. But the charge that abortion is racist is commonplace in the pro-life movement.

If the womb is the most dangerous place for an African American, that makes black women, the victims of racism, the real racists. Put like that it doesn't make much sense. The metaphor ignores the subjectivity of black women; once again, a woman is a vessel, a place—in this case a hostile place. Imagery of abortion as slavery or genocide allows abortion opponents to posture as anti-racists without having to learn anything about the lives of black women or lift a finger to rectify the enormous and ongoing legacy of slavery and segregation. They think that it is easier to just shame black women into giving birth to more children than they feel they can safely bear or care for, and all will be well.

6. Abortion opponents would never punish women

That's what they always say: Women are abortion's "other victim." Only the providers should be charged with a crime. That view would come as news to the many countries where women are in prison for ending their pregnancies.

Right now, putting women on trial for abortion sounds far- fetched, I admit. There's little heart for it in the ranks of the pro-life movement. But the groundwork is being laid. Women have been arrested for self-abortion in several states, although few have been convicted. Many have been arrested and some imprisoned for drug use or other behavior during pregnancy, even when no bad outcome occurred, and even when the law was clearly designed for some other purpose (to protect living children from meth labs, for example). For decades the anti-abortion movement has striven to enshrine in law the view that the embryo and fetus are persons. They won passage of the federal Unborn Victims of Violence Act, which made causing the death of embryos and fetuses a separate crime from the harm caused to the pregnant woman, and versions of that law in many states. In the spring of 2014, despite strenuous objections from women's groups and medical organizations, the Tennessee state legislature passed with bipartisan support, and the moderate Republican governor signed, a bill that would subject to criminal penalties of up to fifteen years in prison drug-using women who had a poor pregnancy outcome.

As abortion becomes restricted, and the embryo and fetus are regarded as legal persons in more and more areas of the law, it becomes increasingly difficult to say why a pregnant woman's conduct during pregnancy should not be subject to legal scrutiny.

Chapter 4

Religious Aspects and Inputs

Anne Hutchinson's experience speaks to a persistent question: What is the source of religious authority? Is it the individual or the community? Who decides? How much dissent can a religious community tolerate? What are the limits, if there are any?"

What I find interesting is that atheists and agnostics know more about Christianity than Christians. U.S. Religious persons know of these occurrences and yet they are constantly battled by those who have now refused to believe in such divine beings.

In my experience, I have come to the realization that most Christians are not really Christian, in the same sense that they don't follow the teachings of the bible. This is probably why they are more culturally Christian than you expect them to be.

They identify as Christians without any thought of following the teachings of Christ, but personal values and views that did not need to understand what it meant about being a religious and devoted person.

Forgiveness and love are the key component of many meditative and contemplative practices, perhaps even as a Christian. The approach can also be illuminating to everyday life. To be mindful is to focus our awareness and attention on the experience of the present moment. We can be mindful of our spiritual sensations and breathe; our thoughts, feelings, speech, and actions; the natural world and our immediate environment; the people around us; and other parts of our lives.

Spirituality practices encourage us to slow down and notice what we can be directly aware of at any given moment of who God is. Many of the teachings recommend that we begin by sitting in a quiet place and noticing the movement of the breath in and out, focusing on the sensations and sounds that let us know we are breathing, and understanding God is a forgiving God.

By bringing your understanding of God to this one simple and flowing experience, we may be able to temporarily let go of our habitual thinking, daily narratives, and worries. Along with formal meditation practices, we can be mindful in our everyday lives. Eating a meal, cleaning, walking, driving, and other seemingly mundane tasks are all opportunities for mindfulness. The more we ground ourselves in the present, the more fully we can experience being alive.

Christian theologians had differing views on the beginnings of life, or a soul, through the years but from one of the more respected thinkers, St Augustine, comes this: "The law does not provide that the act (abortion) pertains to homicide, for there cannot yet be said to be a live soul in a body that lacks sensation."

So historically, there was no hard and fast rule that everyone agreed on as to when a fetus has a soul, or was or is a person.

Be it further let come together, let's call upon religious people around the world to work for legislation to allow the possibility of abortion under such conditions as rape, incest, clear evidence of severe fetal deformity, and carefully ascertained evidence of the likelihood of damage to the emotional, mental, and physical health of the mother.

Abortion Laws are not Constitutional for Women

I am a man, a serving voice of God's teachings, and I wish that this book would serve as a blazing torch to those who are in need of clarity. We have to step out of our cozy boxes and look at the world differently. The reproductive rights of women have been constantly debated about and this is no easy story. The parts of this chapter aim to express the urgency of seeing women as they are, what they are capable of, and the rights that they naturally deserve and yet are constantly undermined. In writing this, I have opted myself to be spiritually guided, well-informed, and socially aware. It is my duty to talk and to do so with fervor. I wish to open the discussion and put the lives of women at the priority table, to be discussed and given importance because respect, appreciation, and empathy are the values I uphold and wish for the world to also foster. In deeming ourselves responsible with each other, I knowingly put this obligation to you all.

As much as we must exercise and enjoy our own rights and privileges, we must not exhaust it to the point wherein others are heavily affected. One's right must not be compromised for the other. This same sense goes along with women's choice to protect and decide for their own bodies. This is not just about the life of a child; this is also about the circumstances faced by the woman. Not everyone has the right resources and circumstances to care for a child, especially if it is unexpected. Even more so it becomes critically difficult to face when the process of becoming pregnant is against the will of the woman (negative implications of men towards women and forced actions to result to this). When we talk about abortion, we talk about such a big decision in a person's life. A choice to keep a baby is in the hands of the mother. It should not be given to the men and the eyes of society who have not taken the time to assess the situation clearly and closely.

No man has the right to condemn women for voicing out, for speaking up, and fighting for their rights. It is the upright and correct thing to do and follow, to support women and their endeavors. Have I not made myself clear enough that you still end up losing your sight of such a notion? If you continue to disrespect and diminish the worth of women for the comfort of your masculinity, your belief, your ego, and your pride, what does that say about you? Most of us find comfort and entertainment in degrading the struggles of women and this is a harsh and bitter truth. But this is a battle of morale and values. When you are a man, you are equally responsible for the safety and protection of women not because society told you to do so but because it is only what is rightful for you to do. This premise does not only apply to women because men also need protection from other men and women. What does this tell us? There is no lesser gender or preference at all. It is not based on that. There are good and bad people, no matter the gender and sexuality. We must not limit ourselves by these propositions and seek beyond our individual selves in order to contribute to a civic society that upholds equal rights for all people from all backgrounds. No one is exempted, everyone undergoes the same judgment of the law, and this also applies to the teachings of our God or whoever being we choose to believe in.

For God so loved the world and He has guided us in all our journey. He is always beside us, reminding us of our core purpose and staying with our sinful selves by continuously showing mercy and forgiveness. Why don't we possess the qualities of a good man? There are some who do, and they are a crucial part of society. But they should not be treated as rare. They should not be a special kind of people. They should be the norm: the stewards of God who emanate and embody good will. It is through charity, respect, and preferential options for the poor that we may be able to dig deep into what we want, into the depths of our hearts. Do not hesitate to count yourself in and strive to belong with these kinds of people. Do not pretend but seek that these qualities will be attributed to your possessions.

When you are a woman, you should feel safe in the home you belong in, in your community, and in your fellow people. The fact that women have to follow such discreet and strict rules among themselves shows to us that we are still faced with the constant restraint of patriarchal society. No man is indeed an island and women should not feel like they are alone in this battle. We owe it to our women to believe in them, to nurture them, and to not take away the rights that they rightfully deserve. In honoring our women, we see them as more than just the bearer of our children. When we see our women, we must be reminded of warmth, of hope, of strength, and of mindfulness for they are the true empaths of the world.

Have faith in the workings of God but do not ever forget that it is your duty and obligation to cultivate yourself. In putting such a strong foundation in your principles, you will be reminded that it is not your call to make when women's bodies are concerned, it is theirs. Abortion is an issue that should not be treated as a taboo in countries. We should encourage and let women from different communities engage in how they could proclaim and promote womanhood better. In preserving and aiming for the betterment of valuing their womanhood in society, the laws and regulations must protect them from being harassed, discriminated, bullied, and even the worst cases of abuse that women go through. No woman deserves to be treated like she is a lesser human because she is totally not. In a closer look, no person ever deserves to be mistreated at all and yet, most women suffer these circumstances.

You can look at the statistics of women involved in such horrifying instances of prejudice, bigotry, intolerance, insults, unfair treatment, and even sexism and rape. Think about it like this, what if the woman you did not treat properly was a friend, a daughter, a sister, an aunt, a mother, and a lover? How would you feel if you were in her shoes? Don't you think they have suffered enough trauma? Abortion is just one of the many challenges she faces beside ignorance. The law sometimes condemns women who choose for themselves a better future. If a woman believes that she is not yet at the right headspace, the right point of life where she is emotionally and financially secured, in an instance where she is much too young and is still in need of marital guidance. How could we pass this obligation on to her when she is not even sure how to take care of herself?

Thousands of women and couples encounter an unwanted pregnancy. If a woman chooses to preserve herself, in whatever choice she makes, we must support her and be with her through every step of the way. Do not be a part of the problem. It will just make things worse. Strive hard to make a difference. Listen to all the voices of the women. There are those who are left unchecked, unguided, and not given the right access to education so they suffer immensely with drawbacks that hinder them from achieving their greatest versions, their fullest potential. Why should we take this away from them when it is a great part of their lives? They do not owe us anything so why should we expect to be cared for by them when we do not even give them the respect that they have long been fighting for? Indeed, we are such a disappointing kind if we push and tolerate such a thing. We are not following the will and the teachings of the Lord if we continue in this worthless journey.

My book was written by first-hand witnesses about women, this means, of course, there is room for factual error. In fact, some mistakes have been carried right up until the present day by most authors – including one detail in particular that women aren't superior to men that is surprising but inaccurate. Yet unfortunate errors can still creep into the information we have about her, and that's partly down to the fact that ignorance was written about women. Then, however, something unexpected happens, and the researchers are forced to seal up their experiment for good. Unsurprisingly, humans are fascinated with lies about her, because lies are easier to believe than the truth. They can go deep below the surface to find out the truth about the earth.

But ever since the first artificial satellite was sent into space in 1957, humans have also been infatuated with looking high up to discover the secrets of the stars. And now, with the help of global space agencies and private companies, we know more about the universe than ever before. But as we continue to stare skywards in wonder, are we overlooking another equally mysterious world back on Earth?

I would like to share this book journey of mine with these lines in which I felt the blissful experiences writing about her. She has a name, an Identity, and is anonymous to some and a mystic to whom they don't understand.

Because of "Ignorance" which is pernicious and dynamic whereby only the symptoms rather than the causes of the maladies are treated.

The questions which I ask myself quite often writing this book, and writing in general, was Who Am I and Why was I chosen to write about women? The questions were so beautifully answered by God that now I feel I have no questions to ask. Everything seems so crystal clear now as I write my 5th book. I know deep in my heart that everything was found in my silence and obedience, when I began deepening my faith by listening which then pulled me closer to my true self and made me realize that the noise external or internal would take me to my ultimate path ordered by God. In order to know yourself and understand the gift given by god, you need to go into deep silence and listen for the quiet still voice of God.

I'm still in awe working with God's given talent to write, I'm still shocked, shaken to the core, my mind still spins to be correct all while the supreme power inside makes adjustments as I write about her and I go with the feelings of being blessed.

I did not know how to react to the feeling, while writing the books, but I felt the supreme inspiration and influence inside of me and sometimes it became numb but I still wrote.

Writing for the first time, I had a true glimpse of my true self and realized who I was and whom I was writing about. Therefore, I closed my eyes to experience and embraced the moment and smiled deeply. I was smiling because I was thinking how close I was to realize the truth about women, it made me realize - she was and is the chosen one, and I was destined to write and write about her. An enormous emotional feeling of immense gratitude engulfed me. OMG!

This is a clear message to those who can benefit from their unselfish actions reading about her. You will be amazed and edified by the raw emotional intensity of words written about her characteristics of womanhood. I was completely blank, fully in control, though I thought answering questions one by one was kind of frozen. In addition, when she asked the last questions in the stories, why was I chosen first and why am I not respected? Tears of sorrow rolled down from my eyes continuously and I closed my eyes, to meditate on God's words given me to write my answer about women.

Oh, I was so ignorant to believe God didn't choose me to write the book and fill it with crucial stories, so I went outside to hear and feel the wind and thank God again. My mind is still occupied from what happened to me in the stories as I wrote one by one.

I imagine looking into Her eyes, she would ask me questions which never crossed my mind about God creating her for humanity-sake.

This man is a simple man like you but the only difference was he was awake with God.

I was silent, cold and frozen in time, astounded still thinking about the experience and suddenly I felt that I merged with everything around and everything merged into me...The people sitting in front of me, those chairs, wood, fire, smoke, ash, trees, sky, stars, earth, me...everything was one.

I felt myself being pulled into nothingness, that void which I felt inside of me in the session. I closed my eyes and felt how nothing and everything at the same time was SHIVA for whom I yearned restlessly.

Chapter 5

A Closer Look at the Struggles of Women

A twelve-year-old girl in Alabama has been raped by a close relative and has become pregnant. The new law forces her to take the pregnancy to term. If she is an average American girl, she weighs 90–100 pounds. She is in sixth or seventh grade. She just got braces. She loves Justin Bieber and she is going to have a baby. She will likely gain 20–30 pounds, assuming she has accessibility to proper nutrition and proper prenatal care. She will likely miss 1–2 years of schooling. She will be a victim of social abuse and stigma as her morals and integrity will be questioned, especially in a heavily Christian state. If she is willing and able to name the father, there will be arrests and constant unrest.

Her little body is going to be changed in ways it is not meant to change. Her stomach will be distorted and skin stretched, her not yet formed breasts will enlarge and likely be permanently altered. Her spine will be asked to carry a load it is not yet prepared for. Her twelve-year-old pelvis will be poorly-sized to cope with delivery.

Her mind will be profoundly disturbed and she will likely suffer from some form of PTSD. Her parents and other relatives may abandon her, blaming her for her rape and bitter at having the responsibility to raise her baby. This is assuming there are capable parents in the first place. She will never be a little girl again. She will bear the constant reminder that her child was not conceived of love but via abuse.

To those who believe that putting the child up for adoption is a solution, just know that all of these things will happen regardless. This little girl will be permanently damaged. I cannot imagine that the idiot ignorant (mostly male) legislators in Georgia and Alabama and elsewhere ever considered the above.

What people do not understand is how hurtful and traumatizing it is to be a woman who undergoes constant ridicule, abandonment, and neglect. Indeed, time has told us that women has acquired several noteworthy rights and changes have been made, but why do women still feel like their reproductive rights and healthcare access are limited and unavailable? In Africa, women are taught to live alongside the insurance of the pleasures of men. As they reach a certain age, they are forced into practices that are deemed to be internationally considered as unlawful and disrespectful to the rights of a woman. There are women who are removed from the right to feel any pleasure at all and these cultures can be found everywhere. It is present in the Middle East and the North African region; it could be everywhere.

Most human trafficking victims, who even result to having unwanted pregnancies and trauma-induced experiences, haven't been given the chance to live a normal life and not be burdened by the life of another child. Statistics would tell us that it is mostly women who are catcalled, harassed, and taken advantage of in public places (the streets, pubs, malls, workplaces, restaurants, recreational facilities, and even schools or universities. It is such a bitter truth that women suffer such unaccepted behavior from men-since they are mostly the perpetrators. If you argue with the fact men get harassed too, then don't you think this is done by the same men? There are men who feel abused and unconsented touching has been a common norm in Arab countries. Cultures seek to create harmony and peace and yet, if we continue to act as if these events do not exist, then we are doomed as the human race.

What did God constantly tell us? He urged us to follow his footsteps of goodness. There is no such thing as a passage that says women should serve the men. There is no such phrase in the scriptures themselves that tells us to shut off our mouths because abortion is allowed in the Bible, you can never find that anywhere. So why are we so keen to prove a point instead of listening to what our women have to say?

In America, healthcare is so expensive. A family has to juggle multiple jobs to afford rent, food, and other necessities. Mothers are burdened to provide for their families, they have that duty just as much as men. So do not ever tell me otherwise that women do not contribute to society because they do, in fact, do well enough in making society a little bit better. We need the temperament of women, their wisdom and empathy to create laws and policies that center on the equality of both men and women, especially with their rights. You must not stay deaf to the cries of the unheard. You must hear them. We must not treat sex education and other sexual health initiatives that promote a healthier approach to women's reproductive health because for years, we have boxed them into identities that suppress their needs.

Babies should not be FORCED to have babies

Edit June 6, 2019: Thank you for the upvote support, 1400 and climbing. Obviously, my answer struck a nerve on both sides of a very divisive issue. I want to note a couple of important things:

Though the scenario cited is fictional, it is representative of real-life cases occurring throughout our nation. I believe that the age and circumstances of any woman wanting to exercise her legal right to abortion are irrelevant. Her body=her consequences=her choice.

I am sure there are myriad examples of women or girls who choose to carry a pregnancy to term against the wishes of parents and/or the father. I believe they deserve the right to make that choice also.

We are the vessel of God and in recognizing this, we see to it that we live by the values he upholds. To care for others, for our women, for their rights. Think of how much love He has given us, the sacrifice and the mercy He has shown to us. As a man, I feel the duty and the burden of being a truly good person. How could I ever face God if I, myself, am taking part in not letting women choose for what is right for their bodies? The pain that women feel is what God sees, what He feels. We are constantly reminded of our path to take and yet, most of the time, we still lose our way.

How unfortunate it is that we do not have enough representation in Congress, in courts, in any body requiring the decision and input of the masses just because an opportunity of a man is vastly different from the opportunity of a woman. Think of all the innovative motions we can attain if we let women lead more, if we let them influence society in realizing what is most important. We are so used to the patriarchal standards that we do not see how much time has changed.

The generations before do not encounter the same challenges as us. And yet, the common thing the past carries to the present is the restraint and holding women down. How many women are expected to take on jobs just because they are female? How long have we waited for women to be able to have an education? The ability to work in whatever occupation she desires? Think of how women leaders are handling the COVID-19 pandemic action, the process of acting fast has resulted in lesser losses in public health, economic crisis, and many more aspects of society. Imagine if these women leaders were a part of the circle of men that society has closed the doors for them for a very long time now. Once those doors are opened fully, without any form of hesitation and doubt, think of how much harmony there could be between men and women. No amount of restriction can stop women from fighting for their bodies.

Far too long we have underestimated them, pushed them down to a lower level because somehow, along the way, we have forgotten the feeling of how much potential they hold and possess. Think of how much the salary differs from men to women. Why do they have so much disparity, with men earning more even when they work on the same job? Even when they started the same way and possess the same qualities? Perhaps even, those women possess more character and passion with outstanding performance for the job but they are held to a minimum level just because of their gender.

How sad is that? Now since you see so much of the disparity wherever we go, think of how patriarchal perceptions stop women from gaining their rights to choose for themselves? Think of the bills and laws passed by the ignorant who do not possess the uterus? The policies presented by the one who chooses to stay blind and ignore the pleas of the women?

It is such a common thing to think that being better than women is cool. But are we really better than them if we have to have that crab mentality? Or are we just scared of the impact women could create to our own society once they gain more influence and control? Why should we be alarmed if we're confident in ourselves and we support these women who just want what's best for society? Why do we have to get a say on whether they choose to have an abortion because they were abused, raped, or worse? Who decided that for us and why do we choose to follow relentlessly? God has expected more of us and even if he is all-loving and all-forgiving, there is only so much he can take if atrocities are targeted towards women who are only trying to live their lives filled with suffocation and neglect.

I chose an extreme example likely to catch the attention of the reader because the law in Alabama was purposely written to force it to be heard by SCOTUS, a thinly-veiled attempt to bypass the legislative process. The pro-life supporters are attempting to force the issue through the Court in order to allow 5 justices to do the job that they know they cannot accomplish through less disingenuous means. The majority of Americans - 58% - support Roe and utilizing the elective process to overturn Roe would fail. Thus, they choose to subvert the will of the people and pursue any means possible to force their opinion upon the majority.

What a beautiful feeling. Trust me this feeling and realization can't be expressed in words but I wish people felt this and realized who they are. I feel calm now, no more restlessness, the past struggles and sufferings have evaporated and I live in the present moment. It takes time to develop this state but it is not strenuous anymore. I can shift my thoughts and come back to the present more often which was a daily struggle for me and I am sure that's with everyone. There were other couple of experiences which I had in the camp that I won't be able to share here but the profound experience I had, I shared it with you all.

I would also like to mention that the camp is held at a very beautiful place in the Himalayas with extremely compassionate and humble people around who will take care of you like their own family. The place is mesmerizing with colorful flowers all over, lots of warmth and sunlight, butterflies, trees and cool breeze, a few enchanting fragrances around that you would never ever forget. You would have to come here and experience the vibes yourself. If you are destined to be here, nothing can stop you. It's not an exaggeration, I am simply expressing what I felt being here.

I do not want to dwell in the past about her struggles, pain or suffering while researching and writing about her as that doesn't hold any significance anymore. Past, just what it is, doesn't exist for her now. All I know is that I was destined to be here at this time and at this moment in my life to write this book. This journey in writing this book changed my life forever and I hope it changes yours too.

Our life lessons can come from anywhere, and who better to give great advice than women? These are women who have gone through many things, and best of all, they oftentimes went to God. The women didn't do interviews or write books based on their own lives so that everyone can learn important lessons from their experiences. But so many authors have learned from their interviews and tell their stories.

When it comes to figuring out famous women's lives, there's nothing better than learning about what inspired them, and I hope my writing has made certain decisions or anything else about her lives.

We know that plenty of our users are writers themselves. You cannot deny that everybody has a story to tell - and there is no better way to tell a story than through a book that can be cherished by the readers for years and years. The way I see it, people can have a sense of relativity in some way throughout exploring the content of this book. I am confident that either you will have a deeper reflection worth the time or you will come to share more of your knowledge to improve the message of this book. Both choices lead to a surprisingly good outcome anyway. I want to let you realize how important it is to know about the rights and choices of women while awakening the desire for true, equal, and evident social justice towards our women. Stand tall and be that pen or paper, I write with vigor so you should be the other end of the string that promulgates the truth of what we should see. In looking upon and stumbling on this book, I wish and hope that an insightful journey awaits you. Indeed, there are so many ways to look at the world, but I do hope that we see it the same way. As long as we come to value our principles, our God, and our women, then we are all seated for a meaningful and fulfilled life.

Chapter 6

Uniqueness of A Perspective

If you've been looking for ways to express your unique perspective and be original, there is no better way to get inspired than through our collection of biographies from famous writers. I do understand that no one would believe that someone could have the impudence to distort the truth if told correctly, but anything is possible. So many things can happen. In order for us to reach a middle ground, a middle point, it is important for us to meet somewhere. Despite our differences in perceptions and beliefs, I do believe that these authors, along with us, share the most important thing that can weigh more than any other: our communal humanity.

Each time I or any author writes about her, she is reborn and seems more present to describe her birth. But I do believe if you asked any woman the circumstances of her birth, she's likely to tell people she had not been born; she had been made by God. But I muster and get the opportunity to live through her experience all over again, as I write because, by doing so, I believe that I may be of use to you, just as I believe you will be helping me on my journey beyond my personal opinionated-opinion. By keeping me lucid, enabling me to put on and to take off at will the mask which shields against ignorance talked about her in others books.

The success of these storylines hangs on briskly and richly to the prompting seed of her life, her hope, and her aims which grows in each and every person. I tried to encompass all the elements of her seed sprouting in your life in all of my books and the stories that envelop these narratives. Every single time, I attempt to write about her. She is reborn, in my thoughts and it seems more present, and more finely attuned to growing into my consciousness, and I hope you are feeling her as well ❤❤❤.

If there's something she wants or needs, she gets to have it one way or another when it can be done and achieved. This is entirely because she isn't doubtful that she wouldn't get it. This mentality should encourage women to know what they want and not settle for the bare minimum, especially for less. She wants everything and everyone to be happy, more so herself on top of that. In this conversation, she would be the center of interest because her needs have to be met just like other people. For centuries and stretching centuries, the big question has always been the same. Is this an exercise, a practice? Or is it real life? Have you ever met someone that seems like they connect with God on a deeper level than most?

It's almost as if you can see the sparkle in their eyes, like they've been with God. If you ask them, they would probably give you some spiritually-induced and emotionally-driven answer like, "God is so good," or "God is good all the time." And He is! But for them, there is most likely a deeper relationship underneath with God that consumes their heart and captures their mind. It is not just about what is on the surface, what we can see. It is even more about the innate nature of her aspirations to be happy, to have control of her own life, and to be able to help others in the process.

There are a few simple things I've learned in my life that always help me stay on track with my devotion to God. Before we begin, let's be clear. Getting close to God is not about a reading plan, a calendar, a set of rituals, or even a prayer closet. It is all about a devoted heart. We can be preached on to and attend several masses and spiritual gatherings every week. But if our hearts are not honestly pure and filled with good will, then what is the entire point as to why we continue to let ourselves believe that it is what a steward of God should do? How do we convince people to live good and honest lives, devoted to God's teachings, if we do not apply it to ourselves from within?

So, while these tips to develop daily devotion might help you invest in habits for intentional time with God, habits cannot replace a personal relationship with Him. In the darkest hours and within closed doors, what do our hearts really seek? Are our actions limited to what can be visibly seen by others? Isn't it better to emanate this goodness when nobody is watching? If you are looking for a simple way to get back on track in communing with God daily, or develop a regular habit of daily devotion, these simple tips found below might help you in a more intimate and devoted journey with God.

It takes Two to Tango

What really miffed me about all the abortion conversations they all seem to have is the truth that shocking happenings involve blaming the women without giving much thought of the situation. Yes, that's my observation and I'm sticking to it because these things happen in reality; women face this discriminating behavior and suffer immensely from it. If you look closely and take the time to get to know the life of a women, you are subjected to knowing the truth more than likely, men are and become more responsible than women because they were chosen to be the gathering and hunter for the family, don't you know and understand the weight of what it takes to be a father? Are you assured that you can just cut ties because you can leave and get away without sharing the same responsibilities as the woman or girl?

If you are offended by this notion, then maybe you have to look closely at yourself. Those who do not fear or hide any unjust actions cannot feel offended by this. Those who do treat women like this must know that it is such an alarming behavior. Women are not objects. They deserve to be respected and appreciated for the contribution that they do. Do not be blinded by the ego that drives you to feel superior towards women because it is not an admirable character. If you so choose to stick at the dominating "aspect" of your male attributes, don't you think defending and protecting women means that you are not any better than them? What made you think that they are not deserving of such respect? Aren't we stewards of God? Why do we keep acting like accepting women and supporting their pursuits is a tainting move on your parts when it doesn't even affect you at all? Are you afraid to discover how much capability women possess at the end of the day? Don't you think we owe that right to believe in what a woman can do to them? To those women?

To Father God, you are the ideal and only viable example for our fathers here on Earth, and we thank You for being who You are in Jesus' name!!! Forgive our fathers who have dropped the ball on being the father despite the fact that You created them to be in the name of Jesus!!! You said no one is perfect but You and You alone know how it is like in this world because it is difficult to even put our fathers equal to You, you knew no sin, you love us unconditionally, and you are a transcendental unfathomable being we look up to and care for.

There is no doubt that there are many men who have more children than they can handle and some of us go lacking in many ways. Do know that we will always look towards You with pride and joy, trust and admiration, for Your guidance to order our steps like You ordered Jesus' steps. Some of us follow our fathers' footsteps and some simply know not what a fathers (man's) way are to follow, being obedient, honoring our parents so our days can be well with us, loving them no matter what, ready to sacrifice our lives to help and save our fathers, we have to turn to You for instructions and there is no way to get men to be right when a wrongful thing has been done to and in front of them by their fathers and or they have been absent. At the end of the day, a boy can never be what he has not seen, give what he has not received, love or live right unless he comes to You and learns the right way to do it, how can we get men to You, Lord our God? We lean and depend on You for Your plans and purposes just to make it from day to day in Jesus' name. We glorify You in all we do in Jesus' name Amen!!!

Reposting from the devotion of the day I don't agree with praying to God like He is or like we talking to our earthly fathers, there is no comparison, God is my Earthly Father just as He is in Heaven!!!

"Men are so dumb about women's process of conceiving. Some believed that with nine women pregnancies, you can get a baby a month."

Don't you see the problem here? Women are more than just their wombs; they are so much more to society if only we choose to see it.

Found below are the newly implemented laws about Abortion, a crucial theme of this book. I wish that you will get to weigh the consequences of implementing this law and that you would reflect upon it.

Law I. Congress shall make a law respecting an establishment's right and of the abandonment of pregnancy of a girl or woman. If your son gets another man, my daughter pregnant or knocked up, the son and the parents of both parents' children are held liable.

Law II. Because you as parents are responsible for your child or children under the age of 18. The parents of the daughter will be able to sue the parents of the son for restitution until the child is

18 or until the child finished college or university. The law will be placed responsibilities on the parents and will curved the need for abortion and give the child a chance to lived.

Law III. Murder is defined as "the unlawful, premeditated killing of one human being by another." Murder is unlawful killing—that is, killing that is done by the judgment of one human being against another, for personal (rather than national) reasons. The Bible condemns murder repeatedly as a characteristic of a wicked society

Law IV. The new laws hopefully can be passed against everything they considered immoral and inhumane, to assist likes abortion. Now, despite the fact that there were billion human beings on earth, no one could have an abortion, unless the baby were deformed or the baby would mean a risk to his or her mother's life.

Everyone had free life insurance and there were thousands of new jobs. There was much bigger punishment against those that would rape, kill, steal… for rapists, it didn't matter whether they were men or women, they would be in jail for years, and that included those people that got other people drunk or drugged people and then took them home and had sex with them.

Those would serve five years in jail. Child-support laws will be more rigid. Now, if someone did not pay child support, they would hunt him or her down, bring him to the county courthouse they were from, and make him or her pay the money owed in full. The law will make It much harder to live in the United States and anywhere in the world now because people can no longer get away with abandonment.

With the help of the mother's, those people would always be brought to justice, no matter how experienced they were at committing crimes and lying.

The past crimes of child support will be brought to light and people will pay. People still try to avoid doing things, but they would pay sooner or later. Even if it takes years to bring that criminal to justice, they would. The same laws governing student loans should be applied and I do believe there would no longer be unsolved crimes anywhere.

Chapter 7

Stories of Women: See the Truth

Stop and listen to women's abortion stories. Listening and storytelling is a way of caring for women. I'm asking you not to focus on whether you are against or in favor of abortion, or against but just give a little bit of your time to stop read these real stories. Would you listen please?

This will be a good argument for the importance of standing up for people everywhere when making choices that affect their own agency in a democracy.

I hope the stories you will remembered, as hopefully represents a significant change in the litigation and advocacy strategies that we pursue in America for the decriminalization of abortion and protection of women's lives.

It is time to for more women to start telling stories, and to ensure that abortion is a part of the public and political debates. I do believe now that telling stories is not enough to guarantee rights, but it is certainly a step towards eventually recognizing them.

The women in the stories have the courage to speak out about support for reproductive rights and to share some of their own story. We live in a crazy world with backlash misogyny preached and practiced in places of power. I stand with you!

Story 1

After I was sure of my daughter being pregnant, I confronted her about it. She was 14 yrs. old and an honor student. I assured her that everything was going to be ok and that we, together, would get through it. I was a single parent at the time and also raising a 5yr. old boy. I went with her to all of her prenatal appointments and became her Lamaze partner. I was there when she gave birth.

The baby's father was never in the picture. He was a boy that she really wasn't involved with other than the pregnancy. I spoke with him and his father. I was confrontational because he was telling all of his friends that it wasn't his child and was also calling her unflattering names.

Typical of a 15 yr. old that didn't know anything about being responsible. After my grandson was born, I quit my job and stayed home to take care of him while she finished school. I am a Certified Early Childhood Educator. She was in the 11th. grade at the time. She continued going to school up until her 8th. month of pregnancy and returned to school a month later after giving birth.

She graduated 3rd. in her class with 4 scholarships. She was an honor student all 4 years of undergrad and graduate president of her graduating class. She then went to grad school and received an MBA. She now owns her own business, (1st. step accounting) an Accounting Firm and also travels extensively representing a major Accounting/Financial Firm. After her 2nd year of college, I told her I would be comfortable with her getting a babysitter and I went back to school to get my degree in Culinary Arts.

My point is that I'm 15 years pregnant. The old are already frightened and need guidance in a big way. How anyone deals with it will set an example as to how she should confront situations that require serious actions. During hard and stressful times children need guidance through situations not being put down or cast away like they're the worst thing in the world. She was a daddy's girl and still is. Her mom freaked when she got pregnant and acted like it was the end of the world. Things happen and how we react to them make all the difference in the world.

Story 2

I would like to ask you not to write my story down. In fact, I will not record it, this is what I can tell you. I am a writer; I wrote my story and would like you to read it. Read just as I wrote it, please.

It was 12 pm and she was still sleeping, maybe dreaming. She dresses up to go out and look for a job. The smell of coffee wakes her up. She stretches her arms, her back, and she yawns. The bed still invites her to stay, her body has been strange for days now, she gets out of bed to pee, to take a shower, to go to college; it was not just another day, she felt her body was someone else's.

On the bus, she felt like everyone was watching. In the classroom, someone talked about bodies and she had to leave. She did not understand why or what for, but she had to, and she did. Once she got back home, she wrote a text on her phone, but did not have the courage to press "send" at that moment, so she decided to go to sleep, woke up an hour later and sent the message: "Go to the drugstore, please." As if he did not understand, but at the same time did, he answered: "Ok, the drugstore?" She could not say anything else, but he went to the drugstore and he bought what had to be bought.

It happened; it was happening. No, we were always so careful, it was not possible, no! She knew it, her body knew it, no! As the days went by, she felt like everybody owned her body except for her. It hurt. She felt the pain, her breasts hurt, feeling it was painful, the pain hurt. Her body was not hers anymore, she had to get it back.

Looks and talks mixed up with the guilt and the pain, saturating that body that she was rejecting. She was resisting. There was a cost to get her life back; listening to the pastor of the local church on Sunday made her mad, it fed the guilt that she was avoiding.

A suitcase and lots of fear. Courage. They traveled. In her country, she found the warmth of women, the warmth that she needed, women and sisters she did not know in an embrace of bellies, wombs, pussies, fallopian tubes, ovaries, souls who had experienced what she felt. To reach a certain calmness. To listen to her own language made her feel safer, but she was not home. She felt like calling her mother, like hearing her father's voice, like hugging her sisters.

She decided to write her father a message while she was at the drugstore: "I miss you, daddy. I have a question to get out of my chest: is there anything that could make you stop loving me if I did it?". She knew she would probably have to wait for his answer because he worked a lot and usually took a long time to text her back, but this time he answered immediately. "Noooo! My love, you are the love of my life, remember your dad's hugs now. Is the young lady doing well?". She sighed, crying, feeling something between anxiety and relief. She needed those words from her father.

He was paying for the pills while telling her that they should buy fruit and water before going to the hotel. A tight hug on a sidewalk of San Telmo warmed up the cold autumn and released the next step. Only the two of them, together as accomplices, overcoming fate, clandestinely. They paid for the best hotel they could afford and made love.

The procedure had been studied, hospitals, addresses; people they could trust were aware; the moment arrived. While her memories came up like a movie, the pain got to her whole body. Calls and words embraced her. The coldness of her country invited her to stay between blankets while she was feeling pain, pain unknown to her so far. Pain not only in the body. Pain from guilt, from clandestinity, from fear in all its forms. Fears she had never felt before. All kinds of images and colors were invading her mind and stealing her undetermined and complex will.

It happened. It was happening. It was intense. As the hours passed by, she felt her body coming back to her, she was slowly recovering it. Along with her intuition, she felt happiness. I made it, we made it! Intense. If she had felt as if her life wasn't hers, now she felt changed, affected, and like she owned it. She had some barbecue and dulce de leche, they went out to see a tango show. Dance, movement, life.

Listening to her body and giving it life was what she did, as she grew with that experience. Untamed intuition guided her. An intense experience that marks us, makes us stop, take our life in our hands, resist, move forward. Plane and inspiration. Going back to the place where she had chosen to live during a cycle of her life. That same place where she was almost locked up while they were looking for the drugstore to buy the pills; she felt inspired to talk about the unbearable. Inspiration that came from that experience that pushed her to produce thoughts about it. It was her present in action.

It was Thursday and she had class. Self-writing. To live and to write. She is not worried about writing a book or a dissertation. She is busy with writing. She feels that she has to do it. She needs to write. She feels that her experience does not stop inviting her to write. She reads a book before she goes to sleep and sees this: "We don't know anything about a body until we know what it can do." Reflective, but very sleepy, she falls asleep smiling and not knowing exactly why. She was never the same.

New life, new day. It was 12 pm and she was still sleeping.

Story 3

I had a child when I was 15, and the one who raised him was my dad. I used to live with him. He had a very troubled relationship with my mom. I was raped by my stepfather when I was 5, then I went through almost 3 years of violence. I had no one to talk to, there was no way to tell anyone about it. So, when I was turning 18 years old, I was trying to rebuild my life after having had the baby whom my father was raising for me. I met a guy at a party who became my boyfriend. He was older. I thought that maybe an older man would understand my whole story.

When I found out that I was pregnant, I ended up telling this boyfriend. I had an ultrasound and found out that I was already a bit more than 3 months pregnant at that point. That was when I lost it. Considering the time, it wasn't his baby, it was probably from some casual thing I had before. How was I supposed to tell my parents that I was pregnant again? And that it wasn't my boyfriend's baby, and I probably got pregnant from a casual thing? My boyfriend told his mother, so I decided to tell them both that, you know, the baby was probably not his child. He said he would support me, but that he wouldn't raise a kid that wasn't his.

His mother came to me. She said I should have an abortion, that I was going to be ok, that this child would be a burden in my life, and I wouldn't be able to keep studying if I had the baby. She said that I should think of my dad, of all the disappointment I had caused him, and that I should not cause him any more disappointment. She even said it wasn't illegal, that it was my choice. She spent an hour talking to me. I had the abortion and ended up in a hospital, bleeding. At the hospital, I couldn't hide it any longer, so I told the truth. I guess they didn't write it down in my chart. Maybe, if they had mentioned it, I would have been arrested, because I was told that the doctor had to report the woman to the police if he found out the truth.

I was there for a week. I was surrounded by women with their newborns, it was horrible. My boyfriend went there to visit and told me how careless I was for not having noticed I was 3 months pregnant, a bit more than 3 months. I didn't feel anything. I didn't feel sick, I felt nothing at all. What I'll never forget is the moment when they sent me out. The moment when the abortion was really done. When the contractions started, I was there at the maternity area of the hospital. I was walking down the halls when everything came out. All the blood came out. I just stood there staring at the floor in the middle of the hospital. People took a while to help me out. Everyone saw it; it wasn't just me there. Even if I wanted to, I couldn't stop staring at what was on the floor, between my feet.

Story 4

I remember that day very clearly. A boyfriend of mine got me pregnant about a month after he had broken up with me. He realized he still loved his ex-girlfriend and left me. Actually, he was seeing both of us for a while, and I was in love with him. If I told him I was pregnant, he would say I had done it on purpose just to make him stay. He would say it was someone else's baby, because we were not dating anymore. He would say it in my face: "Whose baby is it? Because it can't be mine". I asked a friend to go talk to him, and that is what he told her: "I don't even know if it's mine."

So, I was alone, wasn't I? With two kids, an ex-husband, a boyfriend who was also an ex-boyfriend, and pregnant. A friend knew a guy who sold Cytotec. He worked at a drugstore. I waited for my paycheck and bought four pills. I took two and put two. At the time, they cost me R$ 300, almost my whole salary. I don't know how much that would be today. I wouldn't have any more money in case it all went wrong, and it did. The pills were fake. I had to go to the drugstore, face the guy, threaten him that I would tell the owner if he didn't give me new pills. He gave me new ones and they didn't work either.

A week later it started to come out. A smelly liquid came out, and I had a high fever. I will never forget that moment. I was at the bank, waiting in line, and a friend saw me sitting on the floor, almost fainting and bleeding a lot. I couldn't go to a hospital and say what I had done, so she sent me to a nurse who was a trusted friend of hers and who said that he would finish what had to be done.

I went to a moneylender to pay this guy. And it was in some backyard, you know. I did the curettage without anesthesia. He told me that the infection was already in such a serious condition that my life was at risk. The fetus had been dead for some time, when I was trying with the drugs in the previous weeks. He gave me antibiotics and I decided not to take it; I don't even know if I wanted to end up dying at that moment, with all the suffering I was going through. I don't even know what hurt the most, if it was the curettage in the backyard, the days I spent without being able to say anything, or if it was all this fear of the law and the sin around me.

Story 5

I am curious about the stories that people have been telling you. Sometimes, I wonder if they are just like mine, especially if they are stories about young teenagers. I know that we are all different somehow, and each person will bring out different details. But I imagine that most of them are stories of more or less of the same kind. About young teenagers. Yes, I was 15 and I had just begun my sex life. It was my second day doing it with him. He refused to wear a condom and said that he could 'control' himself. I wasn't on the pill; I couldn't, because I was 15 and lived with my mother. If I came home with anything, she would know. If I came home with birth control pills, she would find out very soon.

Well, but he didn't do as he had promised. He didn't pull out. At that moment, he even laughed and said nothing would happen, telling me to go shower and to put vinegar in my vagina. And that was what I did. I put vinegar in my vagina, tried to put it even near the womb, I don't know, but I did, didn't I? At least I guess I did. At that moment, I started to freak out. In less than 15 days, I took some money from my parents at home. I went out to buy a pregnancy test from the drugstore. It came out positive. I couldn't even keep it at home, couldn't throw it out in the trash at home if I didn't want my mother to know, right? Just for you to have an idea, I couldn't do it any differently don't think I could do it any differently. All I knew was that I wouldn't have that child.

My parents are very catholic. They used to go to church every Sunday. My mother was one of those people who could go to another church, in another neighborhood, far away, just to hear a specific priest or a specific church choir. They used to say I had an uncle who was a priest. One of my sisters used to say she wanted to be a nun. At my house, what they used to say about couples who would live together without getting married, (they called it "to get friendly",) was that they were people who lived like prostitutes. They said that women who had sex before marriage were 'lost', wasted.

So, I didn't want to be any of that. Not lost, motor a prostitute, or someone who "got friendly" with someone else, as they used to talk about it in my house. I mean, if my boyfriend wanted to be with me. This was another thing that they used to talk about in my house. I talked to my boyfriend first, and his reaction was to doubt it was true. He said that I was a virgin before I met him and so I wouldn't get pregnant so fast. He said that girls who had just lost their virginity did not get pregnant with a few sexual relations. I have to say that it was horrible to hear all this. It was horrible to hear this in addition to everything I was going through. I was very lonely, I felt very embarrassed. I didn't know who to talk to, who I was going to talk to at school. I thought that I was the only one who was going through something like that. And I kept thinking that everyone would end up talking to my parents, they would end up telling them.

I had a math teacher whom I liked a lot, you know. I built up the courage and went to talk to her. I know it was very risky, but she welcomed me. She told me to go to her house, so we didn't have to talk about it there, at school. I was very good at math. I participated in some competitions, so I could tell my mother that I was going to study mathematics at the teacher's house. When I got there, we talked a lot. Her husband was a doctor. They were the ones who helped me. Nobody ever knew, I never brought up this subject with this math teacher again. It all went very, very smoothly. Today, I am mature, and I am a math researcher. Every year, I bring flowers to the cemetery, to remind myself of the teacher who helped me to be who I am today.

Story 6

I was still just a teenager when I became a mother. The father was a music teacher from my school. He was much older than me. He already had kids; after me, he kept doing the same thing over and over, getting other students pregnant. He's still a musician now, and it seems like none of it stained his career as a teacher.

I had just started college. My son wasn't even 1 year old yet, and I had to struggle with everything I had to do: studying, cleaning up the house, taking care of him, and looking for a job. I lived with my mother at the time, who always provided and made sure we had everything we needed. But she never changed my son's diapers, never tried to help me, you know? I'm grateful to her, but that was the reality in my life. I had to do everything by myself. I was feeling my youth passing me by, both during pregnancy and my son's first year of life. His dad never visited and never provided any support. Years later, I even had to file a lawsuit. And I had to come to terms with it all, you know? Keeping in mind that child support was my son's right.

I met a new guy. He was very nice and went to college with me. We were studying the same thing, and he liked my son. He used to spend hours talking to him, telling him stories, you know, doing everything that was so important for me. The role of someone that is always there, so we can share things and think about his education together. Slowly, he started to show me another side. He started to show a violent side; he changed whenever he drank. I never liked drinking and didn't want that for me. I tried to slowly distance myself from him. I could notice that a sudden break up would not end well. But his violence got worse and worse as he felt we had no future together.

Then, he started to stalk me and threaten me. He went to pick up my son from school without my permission and spent two days with him. I had to go to the police, and I had to revoke his permission to take my son with him from school. And what I heard from the police and the school were questions like, isn't he your boyfriend, someone you brought home? Things were getting worse. And I have to say this: we didn't have the Maria da Penha Act at the time, did we? We just had to go to a normal police station.

Once, I was arriving home from work, and he was waiting for me with a gun. He tried to kill me. He shot me in the lung. I went to the hospital and had to have surgery. All I could think of was my son, all by himself. The bullet wasn't inside my body, it went through me. At the hospital, when I got there, the doctors and the nurses at the emergency room asked me: "He caught you with another man, didn't he? That's why he did it." No. I have to tell them and you that I didn't answer at the time: no, I didn't have anyone else. All I wanted was to get away from that man.

To make my situation even worse, I found out I was pregnant. I've always dreamed about having another kid. I have to be honest, I used to dream about having a daughter. But not at that time, with that man. Not after all I had gone through, after being shot. I needed an abortion soon. Without risking my life and without him knowing about it. I heard about a clinic in another city. I took a plane, which cost me a fortune, and took my son with me. I don't have many memories of that trip or of the procedure. I have no marks on my body; this is not a story I have to tell. I just remember that, when I left there, I was feeling sure that my life would be just me and my son.

Story 7

This story happened about 15 years ago. I was 13, my boyfriend was a little bit older than me. I think he was around 18, I'm not sure; he was my first boyfriend. I had irregular periods, maybe because I was still young. I had just become a grown girl, right? As soon as I found out I was pregnant, he got me the medicine. It was Cytotec. He gave it to me and told me how to use it. And I did everything as he told me to. Not long after I took it, that same night, I started feeling sick. Very, very sick. I'm not exaggerating. I was throwing up and bleeding non-stop. I was going to the bathroom all the time. I was, you know, almost losing consciousness. I didn't really know what was going on.

He went to see me the next morning, and I was even worse. It never crossed our minds that it was time or that it would be good to go to a hospital. He went to school, I stayed home. I stayed home by myself, because my mother used to work as a housekeeper and left very early in the morning. I kept getting worse during the day. In the afternoon, I walked to his school. I was alone. Just left my house and walked there. I needed help. I needed someone to go to the hospital with me. When I got there, I talked to him. I don't remember why anymore, but he couldn't come with me. I had to go by myself. I went from his school to the emergency room — walking, stopping, sitting on the curb, almost passing out. I was bleeding too much already. That's how I got to the emergency room.

At the hospital, people said right away that it was an abortion, that they knew everything, that it was all my fault, and that they didn't like women who had abortions. Remember this: I was 13. They didn't like women who had abortions, I had it coming, it was my fault, and they couldn't do anything to help me. They didn't even give me anything for pain and sent me back home. I walked back home bleeding, dropping the remains that were still inside me, you know? Really having an abortion. I thought I was going to die, because I was bleeding and bleeding, and I had never been to a doctor before. I didn't know how it was. I had never been to a gynecologist in my life. In fact, I was already 20 years old the first time I went to a gynecologist. It was when I got pregnant with my first daughter.

Story 8

I have two abortion stories. I can imagine some people will hear this and say "two!". I don't know if any other woman has told you more than one story, or if I am the only one to tell two different stories here. Yes, two stories. I will talk to you about only one of them today, and I will tell you why. I am from a middle-class family, I had access to information, to contraception. I knew everything a young woman could know about protection, about sexuality.

I was beginning my sex life, only starting to have sexual relationships. This was not the first one, though. He used to wear condoms; you know? And it broke, but he didn't tell me right away. As soon as I knew I was pregnant, as soon as I took the test and found out, I looked for a group in town that offered teenagers some information about sexuality. It was a very nice group. I went there with my boyfriend and told the truth. They advised me and told me an abortion would be illegal. But they also said I could have options and told me where I could talk to a doctor about an abortion.

I went to this doctor. He was a very rude man, and he was very hard on me. I don't remember my gestational age at the time, but he was emphatic when he said: "if you don't come back tomorrow, I won't do it anymore". I left feeling very scared, and decided to tell my mother. She used to work, so I went to her clinic with my boyfriend and we told her everything. My family didn't really approve of my relationship, so she said she would talk to me later at home. She hugged me, supported me, and told me to calm down. When she got home, she said that, ok, it was my decision and she would be there anyway, but first she wanted me to go to the family gynecologist, the one she trusted. And he was a very conservative man, you know? Just imagine how it was at that time. He was very conservative. But he surprised me, because he said: "look, I don't do it, but I know where you can get the medicine and I can guide you over the phone".

My boyfriend went to where he said we could buy the medicine. It was a street fair. He bought it, I took some and put some inside, following the doctor's instructions over the phone. A few days later, nothing happened. My family had planned a short trip with. During the trip, in the car, I started losing blood. There were huge blood clots all over the car seat. My family took me to our family doctor, who prescribed me some tea. They talked to him in a corner. I don't remember, and I didn't really hear them talking, but they told me to go see the other doctor the next day, the doctor who was helping me. I went there. He did an ultrasound and saw that my uterus was clean, I didn't even need curettage.

It didn't take long for me to end this relationship. It was a teenager thing. I had his support, that I can say, and also my mother's. It was only after everything had passed that my mother told me she wanted to talk. She said she was against abortion, and she would never decide to have one. But she also told me that she would support me, as my mother, support me in whatever decision I thought was best for me. I kept thinking about it. About how it is to be a mother, a mother able to support her daughter and her decisions, even if her daughter was just a teenager... decisions that are different from what she believes. And she didn't judge at the time, did she? She didn't impose on me what she thought. That's why I decided that I was going to solve it all on my own when I went through the second experience of abortion. And that's what I did. I never told her, because I wasn't going to impose my decision on her once again.

When I was 16, my mother died of ovarian cancer, and I had to become a mother figure for my little sister. I was the one who had to take responsibility for taking care of her, and it was daunting.

Then, at age 17, I became pregnant. I went to Planned Parenthood, and the staff confirmed my pregnancy. They took care of me. They were extremely compassionate and informative. They explained the different options that were available: I could carry the pregnancy to term and keep the baby; I could give up the baby for adoption; or I could have an abortion.

I decided to terminate the pregnancy because it was the best option for me at the time. Planned Parenthood helped me get funding for the procedure. It was a difficult decision, but I already was a parent to my sister, and I couldn't financially or emotionally provide for another child. I also wanted to finish high school, and my boyfriend was not in a place to be able to raise a child.

Planned Parenthood provided abortion procedures to 327,166 patients last year who had unintended pregnancy or a pregnancy with medical issues, representing 3% of the total number of health services for the year.

My life is better because of my decision. I got to finish high school, and I became a certified nurse assistant. I decided to apply to work at Planned Parenthood because going there as a patient made me want to help other women the way they helped me, and I ended up working there for four and a half years. If I'd been raising a child since the age of 17, I would not have been able to go into the healthcare field.

Six years ago, I became pregnant again — but this time, I was financially stable and emotionally ready to become a parent. This time, my choice was to keep the pregnancy. Today, I'm a proud parent of a little boy and successfully pursuing my career. It's important that abortion remain safe and legal for women.

Story 9

I recently graduated from college, and I'm looking forward to attending medical school and training to become an abortion provider. The thing I'm most excited about is talking with patients and helping them in their health care process. If a patient needs an abortion, I want to be there to help them as a trusted medical advisor.

It doesn't make sense that politicians target abortion for so many state regulations because there's no other medical procedure so heavily regulated outside of the medical community. Only members of the medical community should be able to make these decisions because they're the only ones who understand how our bodies work and who have the knowledge to provide health care.

I arrived at this decision because of my involvement with Planned Parenthood. I turned to Planned Parenthood when I was in high school for birth control. Everyone there — from the front desk staff to the counselor to the doctor — was supportive and respectful. I was able to get control over my really horrible period cramps and also know I could have safer sex and not have to worry about pregnancy when I was in high school. I also became a peer educator in high school, and that changed my life. I learned about queer justice and reproductive justice and how they are intimately connected because they both are about having autonomy over your body and creating the family you want when you want it.

One of my favorite things about Planned Parenthood is the diversity of its staff. When I walked into the health care center the first time, I saw a wide variety of races but also a variety of gender expressions represented in the staff, and that made me so comfortable. It made me feel that Planned Parenthood respected not only its patients but also its employees, and that they encourage and appreciate diversity. I really love that.

Story 10

A 14-year-old girl is raped. She tries to get an abortion. Hospital after hospital turns her away. A Roma woman giving birth is sterilized. She finds out only years later. Her doctor says it was because her people are lazy.

Deciding whether and when to become a parent is one of the most private and important decisions a person can make. For women, in particular, the ability to control decisions pertaining to their reproductive health means they control their own destiny. For this reason, reproductive rights are an essential component of an open society, without which women cannot enjoy full equality.

If Planned Parenthood weren't around and hadn't helped me, I would not be who I am today.

Chapter 8

The Choice of Abortion and its Effects: No more Wasted Time

Here are following stories according to Teen Vogue (2020) that happened when women had the chance to choose for themselves and their bodies:

Daria, 26

I had a surgical abortion two years ago. I guess what stands out about my experience is just how 'normal' getting an abortion can be. How the procedure, frankly, felt less invasive than a standard gynecological visit. I actually had a laugh with some nurses. I learned a lot about my body. I made a playlist for my visit and it helped a lot. I ate ice cream after and went to work less than four hours later.

I often read abortion stories in big publications that have undertones of heavy emotions. I would love for women who are considering having an abortion to hear that sometimes it's just a medically mundane process. And it doesn't always have to be a part of your identity. I always felt guilty that I never considered mine as a significant life event, until I realized I didn't have to.

Veronika, 19

When I was 17, I found out I was pregnant. I knew immediately that I needed to have an abortion. I had just gotten into [college] and was ready to change cities and start working toward a career in electrical engineering. I knew I definitely wasn't ready to start a family. But in my state, the law said I needed my parents' permission to have an abortion. My father is religious and conservative, and I knew I couldn't talk to him about it. I feared what would happen if I told my mom I got pregnant and wanted an abortion. We weren't close and I was scared she would kick me out. The law was forcing this decision for me. I cried because I knew I needed to get an abortion but didn't know how.

I reached out to the nonprofit Jane's Due Process, which helps minors obtain abortions through a judicial bypass. They walked me through the many steps I needed to get through before appearing before the judge, including getting a sonogram and working with my lawyer to compile evidence of my maturity and why I wanted to have an abortion.

I was required by law to prove I was "mature" enough to make the decision. The judge got to decide my entire future, before I was able to make any decisions of my own. I felt so out of control.

Ultimately, the judge ruled in my favor. But I still had to deal with cost and travel, barriers that are harder for young people — especially teenagers — to overcome. In some places, you have to wait for weeks and drive for hours to get an appointment at the nearest clinic. When you add the delay of having to appear before a judge, it's even longer before you can get the abortion, pushing you further into your pregnancy, and making the cost even higher.

Having an abortion was the most responsible thing I did for myself and my future, and I will never regret it. I started sharing my story to try to change parental notification laws and others that threaten abortion access. We all have the right to end a pregnancy if we're not ready to carry it to term — and to make that decision on our own, without parents, lawyers, or judges.

Kenya, 44

At 39 years old, I found out I was pregnant. Without hesitation, my partner and I both knew that an abortion was the best option for us. Being that we were both full-time single parents of teenagers, we were not looking to have more children. I called Houston Women's Clinic and scheduled an appointment. I had gone there for previous abortions so I trusted them. The doctor that performed the abortions also delivered my daughter and provides OB-GYN services to me as well.

On the day of my appointment, I woke up feeling great and sure of my decision. I arrived at the clinic, checked in and started completing the required forms. All of a sudden, the most excruciating pain hit me out of nowhere. I felt faint, I could barely speak, and it was also difficult to get up from my seat. The pain was concentrated on the right side of my uterus and it was unbearable as well as relentless.

They rushed me to have an ultrasound. I remember the ultrasound technician saying she couldn't see the pregnancy but she could see fluid in my uterus. I had no clue what that meant but I would soon learn all about it. The nurse asked me if I was bleeding and responded no. She had me lay down in one of the procedure rooms and held my hand to comfort me. She told me it sounds like I may have an ectopic pregnancy and could be possibly threatening to rupture one of my fallopian tubes. She also stated that it was a life-threatening condition. I started crying even harder because I was all alone. I didn't want to tell my mom or anyone because I was embarrassed to be in this position at my age. I felt like she might be disappointed in me. The nurse assured me that I was going to be okay. She then drew my blood to test my pregnancy hormone levels (HCG) and said the results would reveal if the pregnancy was indeed ectopic, but they wouldn't have them until the next day. So, she made a judgment call and insisted that I go to the ER right away.

I immediately drove myself in pain to the ER with a letter in hand from the clinic stating I had an ectopic pregnancy so I could be expedited. When I arrived at the ER, I was directed to a very long line to be triaged. After what felt like an eon, they called me to go for an ultrasound. It felt as though I was made to wait because the letter, I presented them with had the name of the abortion clinic on it. The technician instructed me to empty my bladder. For the first time I noticed bright red blood. It was eerily silent and she did not say one word. After she finished, they wheeled to a room on the maternity floor. All of a sudden, three female presenting doctors entered my room with very concerned looks on their faces. One of them said I was about to go to emergency surgery because I had an ectopic pregnancy and my right fallopian tube had ruptured and was bleeding internally. Because I'd just eaten, she said I had to be the first patient in line for surgery in the morning. They were going to remove the ruptured tube and perform a D&C, so they admitted me.

I had a successful surgery and I ended up working for the very clinic that saved my life. I saw it as my life's mission to provide the same compassionate care I received that day. I sometimes think what might've happened had I not gone for an abortion. Abortion care providers saved my life and I'll never forget that.

Jen, 41

When I was 19, one day I realized I hadn't had my period in months. I'd recently moved to a new city, and I was on the pill, so I hadn't noticed the change. I took the pregnancy test, and before the pee had dried, I was looking up abortion clinics. It was not a difficult decision, and I did not feel conflict or strife. My grandmother was young when I was born, and I knew I didn't want to continue the generational legacy of young parenthood. At the moment it happened it wasn't even about that — I just knew I didn't want to, and couldn't be, pregnant.

My second abortion was when I was 29. I had a much-wanted one-year-old child and was pregnant with a second, which was also very much wanted. My husband and I were happy and stable and were enjoying growing our family.

I went for a routine prenatal exam, with my pajama-clad toddler in tow. I was not expecting any news, so I didn't have my husband with me. As the nurse practitioner began the ultrasound, I cuddled my kid and waited to see his new sibling for the first time. After some poking and prodding, the NP gave me the sad news: the pregnancy had ended.

I was scheduled for a D&C the next day. I had to wait for the procedure because of laws in my state that require a waiting period between abortion counseling and the procedure. Even though my pregnancy was over, the laws still governed my uterus. When I arrived at the hospital, the provider had to read me a script written by politicians in my state that informed me I was ending a life and I could experience depression or cancer as a result of my decision. The provider explained, "this is bullsh*t, but I still have to tell you this."

The procedure was uneventful, and once again recovery was easy. I became pregnant two weeks later, with my second son, who turned out to be one of the sparkliest, quirkiest blessings I could imagine. I've shared my abortion stories with both my kids, just in the same way I would talk about any hard things in life. It's important to me that they understand the unpredictable shape the world can take and know that neither pregnancy nor loss are a punishment.

Joy*, 38

This is the story of the abortion I never thought I'd have. I had an IUD. Had been the operative word. It somehow went missing in the years since it was placed. I found this out the same day I found out I was pregnant. I was raised in an anti-choice community, and my views have slowly changed over the years. I never thought that I would need an abortion. I thought I was supporting other women. Instead, I am the one who went through very unexpected circumstances and am being supported by a legion of women. If you saw me in the street, you'd never suspect that I too am the face of abortion.

Tara, 26

As I sat hearing the echoing voices of protestors, I strangely began to crave a plate of glorious Southern comfort food to soothe the stress and anxiety that filled me. I knew that the people who sat inside this tiny clinic in North Carolina with me deserved so much better. I sat in a small waiting room with 30 people in hospital gowns who were made to feel afraid and ashamed by the state's anti-choice laws and attempts at suppressing our right to our bodies. Two rounds of counseling, a long waiting list, and a 72-hour waiting period forced upon us were used to produce shame and doubt. The clinic was small with no signs or identifying characteristics, unless you counted the groups of protestors hollering outside. Every nurse tried their best to console the sickest patients—the ones that cried, the ones that vomited. Many of the nurses were tired volunteers. They didn't wear name tags because working at the clinic could threaten their careers in this state.

I watched folks wearing the faded hospital gowns with pride, and wondered if they felt tinges of guilt. I myself clinched my stomach, and pondered for a second if I was making a mistake. The protestors, the long wait, the counseling sessions, the anonymous nurses, the anti-choice rhetoric that filled countless billboards in my state — it was all adding up in my head. Everything around me was telling me I should not be in that room. Yet, there I was. After my procedure I found myself in a popular North Carolina restaurant eating glorious mashed potatoes — a comfort food the South has perfected for moments like this. And as I ate my potatoes, I realized I had no regret about my abortion. I made a decision, for myself, that was right for my life.

Arline, 68

I was 36 and had been using a diaphragm successfully for 16 years. I took birth control pills for the first couple of years I was sexually active, but decided that men needed to be aware that every sex act could result in pregnancy, so I switched to the diaphragm as a political statement, always inserting it in the fellow's presence and sometimes having him participate.

I was so successful in preventing pregnancy that I foolishly, ridiculously decided I must not be fertile and stopped using the diaphragm. And surprise, surprise, within 6 months I found myself knocked up. My periods had always been like clockwork so I suspected early on and was able to arrange for the abortion at the earliest possible time — 7 weeks.

A thing that struck me in the years following was that I, and the other women I knew who had abortions, more or less forgot about them, whereas the only woman I knew back then who gave a baby up for adoption never ceased thinking about him, broke down every year on his birthday and wondered about every child she saw who was her son's age.

Kerri, 40

My husband and I struggled with infertility and were so excited when I finally got pregnant. We had our 12-week ultrasound that went great and the prenatal screening testing revealed no major trisomy's and that we were having a girl. I was so excited I always wanted a daughter. My anatomy scan at 21 weeks told us another story — our maternal fetal medicine doctor told us our daughter had heart and brain abnormalities and a small chest cavity. An amniocentesis revealed our daughter has triploid. Our research and discussion with a genetic counselor told us she was not compatible with life.

My husband and I make the heart-breaking decision to have an abortion and end our much-wanted pregnancy. It is by far the hardest decision we have ever had to make and one we did not take lightly, but we did not want her to suffer. A few days later, I was induced and we got to hold her and spend time with her. She was so beautiful. We named her Anneliese Marie after Anne Frank, in hopes like Anne Frank she would go on living even after her death. Politicians will have people believe abortion, especially [later] abortion is cruel and wrong. It is a necessary right-at any stage of pregnancy and in cases like mine Anneliese was the most loved and most wanted baby. A difficult choice made out of love and compassion.

Emily, 23

In summer 2018, I found out I was pregnant by my husband at 22 years old. I'd been married for nearly two years at that point. I took the pregnancy test a few days after my 22nd birthday and my husband and I knew immediately that we were not fit to welcome a child, due to numerous circumstances but most importantly "we don't want children." At 5 weeks 5 days, I got a surgical abortion.

It felt like a strong period cramp. It was not pleasant. But I would definitely do it again if I had to. I'm working towards sterilization because I don't want children and I don't want to get another abortion. Without that abortion, I would have a nearly 1-year old child, and not be living happy. I'd be in worse debt and my mental health would be much worse than it already is. I'm so thankful for access to safe abortion.

Anne-Marie

My story really began in 1993, when my husband and I decided we would start trying to have a baby. Six years later, after three miscarriages, I was finally excited to have made it to my second trimester of pregnancy. At 17 weeks, we had picked out some names and I was feeling good. We both sat in the doctor's office waiting for our turn for the ultrasound. The biggest problem at that moment was deciding whether we should find out the gender of the baby or not. We finally decided we'd keep the gender a surprise. We went into the room with the ultrasound and as the technician did her measurements, we saw our baby. We were excited and I babbled on a bit, but I couldn't help but notice that the technician did not really wish to engage in any of our conversations and was taking a long time measuring the baby's head. I also noticed a large black spot that filled the inside of the head. Never having had an ultrasound before, I didn't know what it meant. I asked the technician, "What is the black spot in the baby's head?", but she ignored my question.

The doctor came in and told us that the baby had a large fluid-filled sac in the brain and would very likely have extreme brain damage as a result.

The exact diagnosis was Dandy-Walker syndrome. We walked out of the office dazed. We had to get in separate cars: he, to go to work, and me, to go home alone and make some sense out of this unforeseen blow.

After a week of seeing specialists to confirm the severity of the abnormality and speaking to my Episcopal priest about the situation and praying and praying for some clarity, I decided to abort the fetus. I had always been pro-choice, but I didn't ever imagine that I would ever opt to have an abortion.

My procedure went well. I knew one of the risks was that the uterus could be damaged. When I awoke, the first thing I asked was, "Is my uterus ok?" I just wanted to have children so badly. It was painful, but I healed. And two years later, I gave birth to healthy twins.

Miki, 43

The day I found out I was pregnant was six days after my mother had died in my arms from cancer. At the time I was unhealthy to an extreme, both mentally and physically. I had spent the last year caretaking for my mother. I was at all the chemo sessions, at all the doctors' visits, all the procedures, but at night I was abusing myself and putting substances into my body to numb myself and feel free for just a minute. This was 16 years ago; I was 27 years old.

I look back to that time in my life and I have so many mixed emotions. I wish I had never started using drugs, I wish I had been a better daughter to my mother, I wish I had not moved. Maybe she would be alive if I had been a better person. Despite all my feelings of regret, the one decision I have never regretted is having my abortion. I feel that my abortion was my first step to my current path. It was the first empowering life choice that I had made in a very long time.

In the 16 years that have passed, I have tried to forgive myself for my previous failures. I have also used my past to drive my future. I cannot change my past. Without these experiences I went through, I wouldn't even be alive, let alone be a restaurateur and a homeowner. I have confidence in myself that you only gain through failure.

Access to a safe abortion saved my life.

Marie, 30

After having my first child, I asked myself "How can a woman who has brought life into this world possibly be able to have an abortion?" But then, I never thought I would find myself 7 weeks pregnant with an almost three-year-old and nine-month-old. It was a surprise to see the positive test to say the least. The initial shock was a happy one but then I started thinking about how I struggled mentally with my second pregnancy and had finally gotten to a place where I finally felt like myself again after battling postpartum depression and anxiety. As a stay-at-home mom, I knew I wouldn't be able to mentally handle going through with another pregnancy and the taxing newborn phase so quickly after my second. I am still breastfeeding for crying out loud! Like I need one more being pulling energy and fluids, not to mention any sense of self out of me for not just 9 months of pregnancy but another year on top of that. I found out on a Saturday morning, by noon that day I knew I had to have an abortion.

My husband and I went the following Wednesday morning. I cried all morning, I cried during the walk in we had to walk past those awful 'Christian' protesters with their skewed signs depicting 20-week fetuses thrown in dumpsters, tied up in garbage bags, etc. (for the record, at 7 weeks, my embryo was barely a blob of cells, not a screaming crying baby that they had to pull out of my vagina), I cried while filling out paperwork, I cried while waiting for the ultrasound, and while talking to the counselor they provided me.

I wouldn't change what I did. I wouldn't be the mom I am today, caring daily for now 2 toddlers, sacrificing any social life and almost all self-care that is suggested to me. I give everything I am to my children and my husband. And I don't have any regrets in making that decision to take care of my family and myself.

Michele, 55

I had an abortion at the age of 14 in the state of Washington. I was being sexually abused by a cousin and that's how I became pregnant. I had to travel an hour to a Planned Parenthood facility to have the procedure. I never told anyone until I had graduated at the age of 17. I didn't even realize I had been sexually abused until I was in therapy years later.

Barbara, 58

I had two abortions in New Jersey. Each time, I was about 5 weeks pregnant, according to the doctors.

I knew instantly, as soon as I discovered I was pregnant, that I wanted an abortion, there was no question. I wanted nothing to do with the fathers of the babies, both of whom I had dated and had raped me, and one of whom otherwise abused me regularly. I knew that if I had a child I would be tied to those men for the rest of my life. I also did not want to go through the pain of pregnancy and delivery, nor did I want to care for, nor try to financially support a child.

After my second abortion I woke up crying and the doctor was yelling at me for crying. A very nice volunteer came to comfort me. I told her right then and there, on the bed, that I wanted my tubes tied. I was shocked when she told me I would basically have to beg a doctor to do it, that it wasn't really up to me.

Paige, 28

As a parent, I knew immediately that having an abortion was the decision I needed to make, but I didn't realize how difficult it would be to access it in my state. I live in Texas, one of the nation's most restrictive states when it comes to abortions. 24-hour waiting periods, mandatory ultrasounds, state-mandated counseling, and out of pocket costs are all a reality here. We even lost over half of our clinics following the passage of HB2 — which imposed medically unnecessary regulations on providers, or TRAP laws. The clinic I went to didn't have the availability to see me for two weeks, and it took several days after that to have the procedure. And when you're pregnant when you don't want to be, every single day matters.

Navigating the restrictions were difficult, but I was treated with the utmost kindness from the clinic staff — something that led me to later work there as a counselor. The system designed to deter me from making this decision actually had the opposite effect, and more, because I realized there was no end to the lengths lawmakers will go to significantly limit our right to abortion — until it's completely gone. Since my abortion, I've rallied on the Capitol steps and spoken with my local representatives in hopes of a better future. I submitted testimony in favor of the first-of-its-kind (and now approved) $150,000 budget amendment for abortion-related practical support in Travis County, for things like transportation and child-care. I joined We Testify Texas to continue sharing my truth and experiences in hopes of someone else having an easier experience than I did. And I won't stop, because everyone loves someone who's had an abortion.

Nancy, 49

I was a college student in 1994 when I had my abortion. It was the right choice for me because I was single and it was an unplanned pregnancy. I assumed getting my abortion would be a simple doctor's visit but I was wrong. In the state of Ohio, before I could have my "legal" abortion, I had to: listen to the pros & cons of abortion and childbirth via the phone, talk to a biased counselor who struck me as anti-choice, pick up a brochure sponsored by the state on fetal development, and had to wait an additional 24 hours before my procedure to give me time to "think."

The legal hoops I had to jump through to get my" legal" abortion was meant to dissuade me, but instead it just made me more determined to have it. The day of my procedure finally arrived and I was anxious, but not because I was worried about the actual surgery, but because I was told that procedures were being delayed because the physician had to," change her schedule so she wouldn't be killed." What? As a patient, that's not exactly the words you want to hear, that your doctor is being threatened, and could be killed, before you get your legal medical procedure done.

Luckily, the doctor made it in that day, and I had my abortion as scheduled. I was relieved because it was the first time, I really started to take charge of my sexual health and really became aware of how restrictive state abortion policies can affect ordinary women like me.

This experience began my interest in pro-choice politics and led me to become a clinic escort so other women wouldn't have to face what I did.

Jessa, 28

In June 2012, I was in my second of five years at an accelerated college. I was entering the first round of internship interviews and juggling Spring term finals as well. I was stressed to the max but my desire to persevere was extremely strong so I just kept pushing through the whirlwind schedule of study-research-write-interview-research-write-study-interview. It only took three days before my body rebelled and hit me with a wave of shortness of breath and a tightness in my chest. Like any good hypochondriac with access to Web MD, I assumed I was dying. After the fourth of the 10 interviews I had scheduled, I flung myself through the doors of the ER. As it turns out, I was death-free and pregnancy positive.

There was never a doubt in my mind that I was going to have an abortion. Terrifying as that prospect was, reality set in that I was completely unqualified for motherhood at 20 years old. I didn't want my life to be put on hold to be chained to the consequences of a shitty one-night stand. I went to Planned Parenthood the next day and began the process of my abortion. The following week, I would return to the office to receive the Mifepristone that would start the process of a termination and then take a second pill the following day in the safety of my room at my mom's, surrounded by all the comforting stuffed animals and band posters of my youth. The staff at Planned Parenthood were sweet and cordial and never made me question my decision. I was and am still grateful that I had so much control over my abortion, as every person should have the right to.

Erin, 45

I have had four abortions. I never used to talk about them to anyone. When I had to fill out the information sheet at the doctor where they ask how many pregnancies, I would always lie. Even staunchly pro-choice friends made incredibly judgmental remarks about people having more than one abortion. When I began working with Shout Your Abortion a friend told me maybe I should lie and say I only had two, because I'd be hurting my own cause otherwise. I thought I was definitely the only one who had had so many abortions. I was scared of other people's reactions and didn't feel strong enough to deal with them. I also didn't know how I actually felt about my own abortions. When your society is steeped in stigma, shame, and dishonesty, it's challenging to find your real thoughts. Telling the truth works!

I had one abortion with one partner, and three with another partner. The last three all occurred within a two-year timespan. They also happened during a pretty profound period of dissociation and disconnect from my own body, where nothing really felt solid or real. Things felt like they were happening *to* me rather than me being an active participant in my own life. Staying alive from day to day was very much the goal, and I wasn't capable of anything beyond that. I don't mention this because I think it is an excuse or justification for having four abortions, but rather to point out that life is very complicated. There are so many reasons why people have multiple abortions.

Alayna, 28

I took the test in a Starbucks bathroom. I was 17, scared, ashamed, but mostly just pregnant. I knew I wanted an abortion before I even talked to my boyfriend. Beyond the practical reasons not to have a baby, I just didn't want to become a parent. For this pregnancy,

I chose the medical abortion (abortion pill), and [terminated] the pregnancy while hanging out with my boyfriend's mom. She rubbed my back while I puked, then brought me apples and peanut butter, like a child myself.

My second abortion was a secret. I only told two people I was pregnant, and with those people it was never discussed. I had the surgical abortion in the clinic and went to work managing a mayoral campaign immediately after. I didn't want my boss to think I was taking time off during the campaign season, or was one of the types of women who would need an abortion. I'm glad to know now that we are all having abortions and we're fine.

I didn't find out I was pregnant for the third time until about two months in. I was drinking one or two bottles of wine each night, so the morning sickness felt like another in a long string of increasingly bad hangovers. I wasn't sure that I wanted to have the abortion in part because I felt like I didn't deserve another. Maybe this time, I thought, I should just have a kid. I'm glad I didn't because it would still be two more years before I was sober and living the kind of life I wanted.

Recently, my doctor explained that I ovulate while on hormonal birth control, which is why I keep getting pregnant. Abortion is freedom. I am happy, whole and alive because of safe abortion.

Anonymous, 41

I found myself pregnant at the age of 34, and was basically in shock. I had always had an irregular cycle, so I had no way of knowing that a late period meant anything, on top of which I always assumed given my period irregularities and advancing age I would probably have a hard time getting pregnant. I took a test in the bathroom of the office building where I had been working a temp job, and it immediately came up positive. When I told my mother, she basically just said "good, so you're going to have it." She knew I had wanted a child for years, and it was like she could not even conceive of the fact that this might not be the right time for me, and that I had options.

I took 10 days to make my decision. I made one appointment, and canceled it. I searched pro-choice websites, desperate to find stories like mine, stories of women who wanted to be mothers, and were approaching an age where it may be harder to get pregnant in the future, but who also knew that they were not in the right circumstances to have a child at that point in their lives. I knew if I had a child, I would love my child fiercely, but ... it just was not the life I wanted for myself or any future child of mine.

Basically, I deferred my dream to become a mom until I had the kind of life that my child and I both deserved. At the same time, I feel so fortunate that I was able to access care with few restrictions, and it was as easy as a telephone call and showing up to a clinic within a week. I was around 9 weeks pregnant by the time I had my abortion, and I chose a surgical procedure with general anesthesia. The doctor was very caring, and the packed waiting room really brought home to me how desperately needed this right to abortion is for women. The actual procedure itself was nearly painless. The emotional toll it took was definitely harder. It was the right decision, but that did not make it an easy one.

Nicole, 32

I had my abortion last November, on Thanksgiving. I had been a volunteer/patient escort for about a year previous, so when I took a test and realized I was pregnant, I was on the website within minutes. This was not my time, and I never hesitated. I owe Planned Parenthood that confidence, and safety I felt to so easily draw my conclusions. I hadn't been feeling well for days, but being a woman that suffers from PCOS missed periods is commonplace for me. When I could barely get through a boxing class, I picked one up on the way home. I never even got up from the toilet before I saw the result and started crying. My partner ran from the kitchen and held me there. He held me and told me everything would be ok, and helped me gather myself and we headed for the computer. When I called, terrified, the next day I was told [my local clinic] was booked for a month, and I would need to drive almost three hours [to another]. I had to take a day off from a brand-new job. Though I was able to get a quick appointment, I was then forced to go home, as you can't have your procedure the same day as your testing. Instead, you are forced to be pregnant another week or two. That was excruciating to me. The wait. I wore sweats. I withdrew from everyone. I felt disconnected and disgusted by my changing body. I was sick. The wait was probably the cruelest part, aside from the $600 bill, one I saw some women leave not being able to pay.

Luckily for me, I chose a medication abortion, the pills, so I just needed a quick second appointment. [My local clinic] was able to see me for my final appointment. I walked past the protesters, the same ones I'd protected other women from countless times. It was surreal. When my abortion was finally done, in my bathroom at home, the wave of relief was indescribable. A depression, and sadness started to lift, and I felt like a human being again. I felt like me. [My state's] lawmakers fight every day to make it even harder for women like me than it already is.

I have never regretted my decision, and there is no shame in it either.

It was my body. My choice.

Emily

I had an abortion seven years ago in Indiana, and even then, the abortion restrictions in the Midwest were severe. I had to view a medically unnecessary ultrasound, attend mandatory counseling sessions, and travel an hour back and forth several times that month, and walk into a clinic surrounded by protesters telling me I will burn in hell, all to get two pills to terminate my 8–9-week pregnancy— all of that unnecessary trauma for two pills. I knew what I wanted to do and have never regretted my decision, but I had to contend with unnecessary abortion restrictions designed to shame me into changing my mind, or to have to cancel the procedure because of all the financial strain these restrictions caused. As a young woman of 19, I went into debt for one of the safest medical procedures in existence because the Republicans in charge of my state said so—that's not pro-life, it's pro-birth. My abortion saved my life—it let me escape an abusive relationship and go onto marry my soulmate, earn three college degrees, and become the person I was meant to be. I want to be a mother but I want it to happen on my terms, not a bunch of old men who run the government. No one should be forced into parenthood. Abortion is a means of freedom for so many of us—I know it was for me—and it's time society recognizes that 1 in 4 of us who have abortions. It's a normal, safe healthcare procedure and I refuse to be shamed for it ever again.

Alyssa, 36

I had my first abortion when I was 20 years old. As soon as I found out I was pregnant I knew without hesitation that I would have an abortion. It was 2003, and my relative privilege afforded me the knowledge that it would be easy for me, while my healthcare coverage assured me, I would suffer no financial strain as a result. The entire experience was wonderful. I was a nervous kid who had no idea what to expect, and I was treated with nothing but absolute respect by everyone from the receptionist to the doctor to the nurses in post-op. A highlight of the day, which doesn't always amuse people when I tell this story, was joking around with the anesthesiologist before I started counting backwards about how he'd better not steal all my stuff while I was asleep. It's been over 16 years, and I can confidently say that in that time I have never once had a more positive, affirming, and comfortable experience in a healthcare setting than I did that day.

My second abortion was almost exactly two years later. This time I went to Planned Parenthood and received the abortion pills. Nobody joked around with me this time, which was a little disappointing because jokes help my nerves, but overall, it was a positive experience with lasting effects. The folks at PP got me on birth control right away and I went on to return to them for my reproductive care for 5 more years, receiving education and treatment which prevented me from having to ever have another abortion.

I'll always be grateful to have been allowed to participate in determining what was best for my reproductive healthcare at a young age; it set the stage for me to appropriately advocate for myself medically for the rest of my life, which is something a lot of people never learn to do.

Amanda, 42

I was 21 the first time I got pregnant. I'd immediately felt certain that I'd have this baby and all would be well, and I was right about that. I was in college then, and the pregnancy itself was no easy road. It was during that experience of being young and afraid of a million unknowns, while also being fully supported by a loving family and partner, that I truly understood why others could not make the choice I had. I felt wildly connected to those who'd chosen abortion even though I hadn't chosen it for myself.

I now have five children total, two adopted. That unplanned baby of my youth is heading into her first year of college. Her father and I have divorced and every idea I've ever had about what my life would look like is ash now. I have a new boyfriend and I'm at least six weeks along before I even know I'm pregnant but I don't for a second think that all will be well this time. I'm self-employed and underinsured. I have no paid time off and my responsibilities as a mom are already sometimes more than I can hold. I surely cannot hold another and I know this in my bones. To end this pregnancy, I drive past protesters holding signs that suggest I don't know what I'm about to do, but I do know. The lengths I would go to save myself and the children I already have are immeasurable. Afterwards, I am relieved and I am grateful and I am again wildly connected, this time to those who want to or need to, but cannot, make this choice.

Poppy

I found out I was pregnant on Saturday September 26, 2015 and had an abortion the following Tuesday, September 29. I was 24 years old at the time and in a relationship with a man considerably older than me who I currently don't speak with anymore. Between finding out I was pregnant and having my abortion, I only told him and one other person (my costar in the play I was in at the time) and no one else. The logistics of my abortion were easy because I was financially stable and was able to make an appointment at the Planned Parenthood quickly. But I also felt really lonely which was a feeling that surprised me as someone who has always been very pro-choice.

I opted for the procedure; the wait was several hours long but the procedure turned out to not be as painful as I had thought. My partner at the time waited in the waiting room and brought me food afterwards. I felt lucky that my partner was there but when I saw him, I felt lonelier than ever. I wanted to call my mom so badly but I was afraid of what she would say, especially because she didn't like our relationship.

Summer, 20

When I was 19, I chose to undergo corrective underbite jaw surgery. Before the surgery, I had to pee in a cup for them to test for pregnancy. Standard procedure. In the operating room the nurse said "the patient is not pregnant." I said "thank God" out loud and then I proceeded to have my surgery. Recovering was not easy but I noticed I missed my period and I figured it was due to the pain medicine and stress on my body from a major surgery. Later I started getting really worried and I took a pregnancy test, I prepared myself for what I already knew was happening. I looked at the positive pregnancy test and I broke down in my bathroom. I was not ready to be a mom, I didn't even think I wanted a baby. I want to go to medical school and be a doctor, not be a mom that struggles to feed her baby. I told my boyfriend of 2 years and we cried together because we really did want to keep it and love it. But we both knew we weren't ready mentally or financially. I worried that due to me being put under for surgery and being on many pain meds it would have harmed the baby. Eventually I booked an appointment for a medical abortion and we drove three hours to the office. We waited about three hours and the doctor gave me a pill to take then to stop the pregnancy, and 4 pills to insert 24 hours later to cause the bleeding and expelling. No one tells you that it's similar to a miscarriage and that miscarriages can be very painful. But the next day I was fine, it was like I was having a very heavy period and then I went back to normal. I didn't regret anything.

Fast forward to March and I ran out of birth control. I had my period at the end of March and I thought everything was fine, until I did not get my period for April. I quickly took a pregnancy test and it was positive yet again. I was just shocked at how easily I got pregnant while so many women struggle to get pregnant. I felt like a complete asshole because I already knew I couldn't keep my baby even though this time it really killed me to think about not keeping it. I booked an appointment at an office five hours away to get a surgical abortion. I was terrified.

This time really messed me up and I definitely feel really guilty. It's not even been a week since I got it and I'm hoping it eases up. I told a few friends about the first one and I told no one about the second fearing judgement and it's been really hard but I do not regret it because I know this is what's best for me. When I am ready for a baby, I want to be able to spoil my little angel and not be forced into having it due to lack of choice, struggling to make it by.

Chapter 9

Educational Approach

Education is about so much more than just reading, writing, and arithmetic. Good teachers help students learn how to think critically, read broadly, and dig deeper to understand the complexities of our world when it comes to women rights. I hope everyone is educated enough to learn that knowledge comes in many forms, and it is not bound to any particular age group or demographic. As Albert Einstein once said, "Education is what remains after one has forgotten what one has learned in school."

On a personal level, education is what enables us to make thoughtful decisions about our own lives, and to maintain an open mind about other cultures, contexts, and other ways of thinking. On a societal level, education encourages dialogue and problem-solving by equipping members of a community with the tools and skillset to imagine new possibilities but sometimes ignorance replaces understanding others.

There is no doubtful aspect about the fact that education seeps into our lives as a possession that can never be taken away. You can be anywhere in the world; you can be anyone else. No one would ever expect you to be someone you're not, especially when you are bound by moral values and with education as well. No one can ever take wisdom from you, especially if you have pondered and worked through years of school and learned the right manners, behaviors, and principles that do not only make you intellectually aware but also respectful and well-mannered.

If only we take the chance to teach our children early on that women are not any lesser, that crying can be okay for a man or a boy. Society taught us to be tough. It boxed us into this mentality that men have to be tough all the time, not showing any remorse or emotion, while women are seen as the frail and weak kind that has to be controlled and watched over the whole time.

In having the cognitive abilities to understand the world a little better, there is no such thing as a lack of growth. When one is always striving to see the world through a bigger lens of understanding, then we can have a bright future ahead of us. We must teach our men and women to prosper in their beliefs, stand for what is right, and treat each other equally. That approach is what God would have wanted for us. He did not teach us to commit unlawful deeds, to discriminate against our women, but He did allow us to reflect on the fact it is our doing and actions that will skyrocket to goodness or forgiveness. Do not be swept away by what is trendy and up-to-date. Be aware of what is happening and see to it that you are not trampling on anyone as you live out your life. If you are an educated person, you must never forget that it is not the basis for a good and purposeful man. The true nature of a good person is not the smartest or the richest. It is the one who finds both marvel attributes to wisdom and kindness all at once. No amount of education can inspire you to be a better person if you do not do it yourself. Only you can be a catalyst and changer of how the world sees and perceives women. If we work our way into treating women as equals, respect and dignity in harmony with our actions, then our world will not only be better but closer to the Lord our God as well.

The Early stages

One of the things about growing up is the fact that you have to learn that bad choices have bad consequences; and although God will forgive you, how you get out of those consequences is a crucial part to your vocation. Of course, for you, one of the biggest challenges is what to do on the day of the awakening - to have life in you be taken from you. I'm not the judge nor the jury, I'm just a man trying to teach and learn why a man gets to choose life over death for her choice. Everyone has their opinionated view on both choices but this time, you are the one that decides on life or death.

Let's make this crystal clear and why should you listen to me anyway. I'm a man and we should not have an opinion on a woman's body. Last time I checked, both religious and scientist/medical men cannot carry a child. They can share their input but never impose a decision on a woman, it is not their place to do so.

Early stage is about planning and becoming knowledgeable about your mind, body and soul and understanding how important your life and this decision is to you and the unborn.

If your only argument is the fact that the only true birth control is not having sex, then tell me, if a woman became pregnant then what can she or you do?

God doesn't charge people a fee to use His tools to make contact with Him. He doesn't run annoying commercial advertisements because His words speak and stand on their own. He is not influenced by powerful corporate interests or elected officials, because he is all powerful, all knowing, and all forgiving. He is here so you can have a say and make a real difference in the decision you are about to make. Please don't brush him off and ignore what I'm saying. If you just listen to what really feels right, then consider that what you are about to do will always be with you and so will God and your unborn.

He will always be free and independent for He does not make decisions that can potentially hurt others. It has always been our mission in life to rely on the generosity of our God. He wouldn't want it any other way because that is what true people power for GOD looks like. The cause and effect or maybe not understanding the consequences of your indecisiveness action can lead to a certain reaction. Here's what they are.

It could be that you:

Took away their faces, took away their families, took away their pulses and their beating hearts, took away their minds and not only dehumanized them but killed them.

You say it is your right but it's your right to choose what is best for a woman? But it's her truth to bear, not man because who made you the caretaker over her. All women have a choice over their body which means she alone decides what should happen in the chamber of sanctity in her body.

The truth is there is no right or wrong answer. The best possible approach is prevention and intervention. I'm sure very few women plan on abortions of their child. My personal opinion is that if more than one child is aborted without medical reason, rape or incest or any form of sexual non acceptance, I feel it is a wrongful act against God and woman. Abortion is not a form of birth control in my opinionated opinion but allows the woman to ask herself, am I ready to become a mother?

There are not many elements of this that must be considered, only one in my opinion: her choice. Her choice affects her more than others as it's a very complex decision, but she may have to face and deal with it. Because of the many different ideas man has about what a woman should do with her body, it may only continue to divide us all into chaos.

SILENT SCREAMS

God said it, I believe it, and that settles it."

Know who she is?

The title read, "Abortion a painful choice," to reflect a personal belief is consequential. The proponents of this book view caricaturize that the woman is divinely dictated in my book of statutes whose truth is crystal clear to anyone who has sense enough to simply read. Of course, I honestly hope to clarify their emotional trials and tribulations with what they called "truth", their views of the truth, shaped by unique sets of circumstances, experiences, and presuppositions.

I know I will often encounter fervent, sincere, Bible-believing people who say things like, "you can't be a Christian around here." I don't disagree, but the sense I get is that some people really want their interpretations of the Bible to be upheld, validated, and shouted at everyone else listening. Now it's my turn to shout out loud, ``judge not or thy will be judged, Love thy neighbor as yourself"!

With this book, I'm trying to be helpful by educating society on Abortion rights for women and young ladies to refresh or to reset and be supportive. When you love someone, you embrace that person's wild oppositional complexity, seemingly paradoxical behavior makes you love your friend all the more.

The key word is loving thy neighbor as yourself! The world, our world, is entered into, intertwined with God's purposes given us free will to choose. Human existence is good and therefore ought to be embraced and improved" (people on top always think that). That's because we all are individuals and we have the right to choose.

Today, women, of whom I have always loved, respected, adored, are asked way too much, especially given up control of their body in a world which is becoming smaller, centralized on ignorance when it comes to women's bodies. Understand that not everyone could be born a woman, but being a good parent or dutiful child could be just as nourishing to the soul and important to a peaceful existence for humanity.

Women's happiness came not through gluttony and self-indulgence, but through frugality and duty to others. She believed fulfilling the needs of others could also fill oneself with serenity and gratitude. Forgoing her duty to be of service to her family, on the other hand, could have wider supporting effects.

Being a Christian, the most famous sayings has been echoed through the ages, often referred to as the "Golden Rule," and phrased in English as "do unto others as you would have them do unto you." The basic principle of treating others the way we wish to be treated is found across the world's religions, cultures, and ethical theories today. She understands the needs of some abortion which might unbalance people's way of thinking and suffer a reign beset with natural way someone thinking.

As my book begins to move into shaping or reshaping society, communities, neighborhoods in schools we see children growing up knowing they have the right to choose. Education seeks to build equity in children and therefore in this country, I am researching, conversing with women, exploring their roles as women to be encouraged and teach children how to pray and prepare for the world.

I am building foundations of knowledge, insight, and truths of what I know about women, the women who raised me, to be courageously driven by her. Women no longer lived in 1921 but in 2021, it's not her fault you have been sleeping.

The women are the cornerstones of our lives; they are God chosen, who are the original matriarchs, the warriors even at times when a patriarchal Africa seemed to be fully ruled by (African) men. But you are trying to take away her rights to choose what should happen with her body.

For past reflection, and reference, my earliest pieces of writing a black man book dedicated to women, mind, body, and soul entitlements to make sure they are protected, prepared and preserved.

Several poems I wrote inspired me to write this book. Silent scream, my little raindrops, but we do not see that — society. We want the tired, the tortured, the tried Black woman to always be at her best. Despite society's needs of Black women, these incredible human beings keep on going.

There is no stopping a woman when she cares, because she loves. It is the most beautiful thing when you see her in action with this focus on family. I have seen it in my mother for a long time.

I can only hope I have given women's half the love, the love caring back to her in my book she has provided me throughout the years. Women continuously deserve so much more than this world is giving to her. Rove V Wade is a great place to stand and start.

Christian Evangelist, well-meaning religious folk are forever trying to over spiritualize God, filling the faith with helium and floating it up toward never-never-land with their own personal choice.

Here's what can be done to support and help women:

Do not reverse Roe V Wade and stop trying to control women's bodies. Women's Equal Pay Day just passed on August 3rd. It is still time to reach deep into this world's consciousness when it comes to economics to pay the Black woman what she is truly worth.

This does not mean going broke to do so, but honoring women for all of what they bring to the table: their life's experiences, the discrimination, the college degrees and PhD's they pursue, sexist or racist experiences they have in the workplace. Companies and corporations owe women equity for all they bring to the table, all of the things they continue to invent, all of what they design, all of what they patent.

As a connector and as an advocate on LinkedIn, it is an honor, a pleasure to meet women on that platform. A lot of them are doing amazing things as business owners, entrepreneurs, engineers, doctors, lawyers, soldiers, airmen, Marines and Navy, coast guard, coders, writers.

Reading their bios or visiting their websites has taught me a ton in the past few year's women are accomplishing more than we give them credit for. Therefore, I'm sure she can decide on her body.

They are doing it in ways we cannot ignore but you are trying to control women's right to choose for her body, get real Women! Women, we owe you everything, and then some. We owe you time, attention, hugs, shoulders to lean on, tissue for your tears of pain or progress, understanding, gentle words, kindness, respect, room to let her hair down and just be a woman.

She knows the world is her mirror for upcoming young ladies. We should be able to look back at you reflecting the beauty, power she possesses. This world, a lot of it, owes you apologies. It owes you sympathy. It owes you empathy. This world should be writing songs for you. I'm writing this book in women's support How amazing you are.

You do owe her much more than you have already given. What we think you owe us is wrong. You have given your heart, your soul all we need to be who we are. We can think all we want to.

But her given power has strengthened entire villages, communities, neighborhoods, cities, states, countries. Many women deserve a break, a breath, a seat, a walk in the park, a vacation. We owe her our support, prayers, wishes, thoughts, love, and understandingly her choice. In fact, it's often when we push past that initial resistance of ourselves, we stumble upon something truly wondrous.

Chapter 10

In Closing a Final Note

As a child, I would breathe against my bedroom window and trace a door in the condensation, through which I would escape in the imagination of being an adult. Now I breathe against the bedroom window and trace a door in the condensation, and escape in my imagination to be a child once again!

I will be the one to follow behind you in your footsteps for women rights to choose, won't you? Be the "someone" that starts helping the victims, one person stepping forward to do what is right, is the right thing in the beginning. We need everyone to change the world. For if nobody starts, who then can follow us?

In the midst of it all, I am faced by thoughts of other people, how they played a part in crafting the ideas of this book. Indeed, I am partly grateful for them and their progressive notions. This certain occurrence has me wondering what could happen to this world full of debates and various beliefs. Now here we are, faced yet again with the adversity regarding women and abortion.

"WASHINGTON (AP) — Both sides are telling the Supreme Court there's no middle ground in Wednesday's showdown over abortion. The justices can either reaffirm the constitutional right to an abortion or wipe it away altogether. 2 December 2021.

Roe v. Wade, the landmark 1973 ruling that declared a nationwide right to abortion, is facing its most serious challenge in 30 years in front of a court with a 6-3 conservative majority that has been remade by three appointees of President Donald Trump".

Friend—As we reflect on the state of our democracy, women rights is part of democracy. I'm filled with both concern and hope. Concern because Roe vs Wade is under attack once again and women's rights to have control over her body is continuing suppression to pose a threat. And hope because I believe that, together, we can put power back in the hands of voters where it belongs. I know it's the holiday season, so I wouldn't ask unless I really thought it would make a difference: we need to come together and support Roe vs Wade!"

Comfort Zone

Most people are against Roe Vs Wade because they are thinking for themselves and taking them out of their comfort zone. They choose situations, choices, decisions that are easy and safe. Because these people permanently strive for personal comfort, security, pleasantness, but lack of personal responsibility. Their lack of effort, but for the price of someone's personal choice. They will need to choose carefully because what they want to do is disrupt your life while comforting their lives. The comfort zone folks don't want or like more comfort or growth, because they can't have both at the same time. If you choose growth, they will get out of their comfort zone

The Bible is clear: since God is the Creator of human life, only God can determine who lives or dies. And every person who claims the name of Christ has the obligation to make certain his or her views line up with His Word. Is it possible for a born-again Christian to be pro-choice? Yes. Is it likely that such a person will remain pro-choice? I'm hoping after reading my book, he or she is allowing

Word to transform and renew his or her mind. The woman is the birth of life, shouldn't she have the right to choose?

In my book, I'm hoping to focus on building connections across issues and choices which divide the communities of people. This one reason the book offers an important model for women rights and reproduction rights—and has valuable lessons to teach about how to support women rights is reproductive rights. Early in my book, I tried to convey that women need more people to help properly fight for themselves and others when it comes to reproductive rights and health care for all women.

There are many complaints about women's rights to choose whether they are trying to be overlooked or being overlooked. This concerned me and others; because they called themselves Christian's evangelist, but they are straddle the fence, and continually to pray and ministry the Word, of how abortion isn't right instead of love thy neighbor as yourself, and forgiveness is for all believe.

Today, if we're uncertain about our career path or job, we can know that we already have half of our job description: to pray continually.

This means we devote whatever we do to the Lord and complete all our tasks in a way that honors God. It also means that we should seek clarity about our role in the world. God had appointed the apostles to preach, but they had to seek Him and talk amongst themselves to find a solution to this problem that didn't take away from their time. God provided other men whom He had appointed to oversee the money. One man was not meant to do everything; each person had a pivotal role in the body. When we call out to the Lord for clarity about our role, He will provide it in His time.

Each of us has a role to play, and the most important role that we have is to be prayerful about everything. We can rest knowing that

He will show us the next steps in His perfect timing and that He will always give the direction we need.

"The world is broken because power and love should have always belonged to women"

"Learn to get in touch with the silence within yourself, and know that everything in life has purpose. There are no mistakes, no coincidences, all events are blessings given to us to learn from." Elisabeth Kubler Ross

Women should continue to fight for the right to decide on their body, become an activist. I have demeaned myself as a good Christian rather than a normal man and a man would rather be a Sower than a Christian.

What good can we do when we constrain them, malign them, and judge them? When we deny them from reproductive health care and force them underground for reproductive health care services, how can that help? We should use love towards someone else's choices. If they are different from your own, what does that matter? Are we not all good people believing in God?

Although women have been more or less misunderstood since Eve and Adam, they are still counterintuitive. She is one thing that's hard to wrap your head around, Adam's would say but once you do, she makes perfect sense.

This is what enabled me to utter such words as these: "Here she stands* we cannot do otherwise. God help us. Amen."

Analogy of pregnancy from a man's point of view.

For you or me who isn't pregnant trying to understand why a woman or young lady decides to abort her child or not. I used the analog of the pregnant mom like boarding an airplane, she is trapped on all choices or decisions she makes. In case of a cabin pressure emergency, put on your own mask first before assisting others, even your child or children. This goes totally against motherly instincts because her first instinct is to protect her child or children. But maybe in this particular situation she has to protect both.

Sounds improbable though, doesn't it? It will just take a minute or two to at least change your mind. Easy for you to say you're not in her shoes. I do believe in most cases her choice was not rushed, many times I believe she asked herself why should I continue or stop until she loses Consciousness of reality.

I think moms are in a Time of Useful Consciousness, and none Useful Consciousness which means a mother's time to think about how long before she isn't thinking correctly or even thinking at all. She's in a transformation stage or being someone else or someplace else.

"Most definitely!" And, "Maybe so." Yes, the intern decisiveness Zone exists in her mind. So, it's a different kind of dimension in my opinion for all pregnant women where they are in a conference with themselves and experience or choices which need to be contained in reality.

So, I try to describes her choice such vague, nebulous terms of transitional format of survivability after the abortion process or not going through with the process is her choice.

In closing this part of the book, it's making sense now, beneath the level of seeing and in the level of knowing. Everything that your daughters are going through, that your mother and sister are going through, and you are going through, is your path to understand the God in you. To all the women of the world, you must live your life to your expectations, not to those or others, and no single description of you is valid unless the validation is of God.

My dear readers I have a beginning -of-year challenge for you: just chip in your support for Roe V Wade. We talk about big goals all the time to support reproductive health care. But the thing we need right now is for more people to be invested in this fight for fair reproductive health care services going into 2022.

We need a greater number of supporters fueling this movement for women and young ladies to make decisions on their bodies. It is a far better indicator of success in a moment if we come together. It's always public involvement or the voice of the people that strikes fear into the hearts of our opposition or the Nae Sauer. This is why they want to limit your access to the ballot box, by limiting your voice, reduce public hearings, put up obstacles to comment and ultimately eliminate competitive elections. We can't let them get away with these attacks on the reproductive health care services processes.

We'd come to the end of the first part of the book but on the contrary, to understand their choice, they should receive forgiveness beforehand and anything whatever about God's fellow servant. From this we see that there are two kinds of forgiveness. The forgiveness of God and forgiveness of humanity is that which we receive from God is that which we should exercise by bearing no ill will to any upon earth. God is the ruler over scoundrels who do not recognize their sins and mock and carry their heads high. That is why the emperor carries a sword, a sign of blood and not of peace. But Christ's kingdom is for the troubled conscience.

If you have any valuable opinion or advice, about what you have read please share with others. What we need is more communication. And if you think more people should read this book, share it on social media and with your friends and family. Disclaimer: This book part is only meant for informational and educational purposes.

Throughout history, men have developed some creative theories to understand women's bodies. The scientific research says a female body bled, bloated, gave birth, and produced milk. That had to be some abnormality but they didn't know God.

Much of this misinformation was born out of the ignorance that fed stupidity. If men couldn't dissect female bodies, they couldn't understand female bodies but I believe they tried and still today can't understand her.

Unfortunately, ignorance also caused fear today in them. And when people have fear in their hearts, it plants the seed of hate and hate mutates.

God says, "I do not ask of you a penny, only this, that you do the same for your neighbor." And the lord in the parable does not tell the servant to find a monastery, but simply that they should have mercy on his fellow servants.

I'm really closing the first part of the book of three books to say: I'm blessed to write this. We all are individuals, and We need to take care of each other. Our biggest enemy is not external but internal because we are not caring and respecting everyone as human beings. And do the right thing to help each other not to cause harm or shame upon them.

Tell the truth, if it hurts!

I don't have all the answers and I'm sure leaving you with more questions than answers at least we are communicating. Focus on uplifting the one's most vulnerable, and respect others in their own bodies.

You cannot do all the good the world needs, but you can do your part. All is good, only if we make it good!

Now you may be walking through each day without clear guidance, an accurate mapping of the choice you made. You need to find a consistent light source for instance, spiritual, religious, counseling or just talking to a person you trust to seek help if not could be hazardous to your well-being. Fortunately, God's Word and book like mine are intended to provide us with the tools and help that we need.

Now, I am here sitting in the waiting room but whatever I chooses it's my choice, I have to live with for the rest of my life.

Thank you, Father, for the privilege of knowing the truth and following it, help us Father never to stray from the parts of truth, help us to set our hearts on your law. Father for some of our families that have not known this part of truth please give them the understanding of the way of the truth which is Jesus Christ your Son. Thank you, Father God', in your mighty name we pray amen.

"God said it, I wrote it, I believe it, and that settles it."

By Socrates Quotes

"The hour of departure has arrived, and we go our separate ways, I to die, and you to live. Which of these two is better only God knows".

"An unexamined life is not worth living".

Meaning of—"Through this statement, Socrates means that an unexamined human life is deprived of the meaning and purpose of existence. To become fully human means to use our highly developed faculty of thought to raise our existence above that of mere beasts."

I am closing part one book of three with this poem:

Titled

Who am I?

Am I the voice with a word; or a person who wants to be heard?
Am I a person with a vision in a dream; or just a person wants to be seen?
Am I a person building and keep the Faith; or a Christians who lost his way?
Am I a person without sin, if I was, I would not need HIM?

Am I a person without God?
Is lost
I'm the one who will pay the cost

Am I a person without a heart?
Am I a bad or good who am from the start?

Am I a flower without scent or person GOD sent?

Am I the soul without God remains unsatisfied?
Am I the soul that has to hide?

Am I the soul who cannot attain peace, bliss and salvation?
Am I the person who are lost in my creation?

In your eyes who and What do you see can you find HOPE in your peace.

What I Am supposed to be, please Let God be the judge of me.

Now you have read my book, we have spent time with each other and now you can trust me. See God's words come in many different ways and in God's words is saying to trust GOD even if you don't understand.

It's my hope and belief that words here will strengthen the connection, by validating each other's choices and opinions. That inspires us in difficult times, reminding us of the valuable things in life, is respect and love for each other.

If more people could simply mind their own businesses, the world would be a much better place, her body her choice?

"Sometimes you need to see beyond your own existence, to know who you really are".

Richard Dexter Russell

"Paranoid is their only defensive weapon"

So, if you drop the baton, pick it up and pass it on to the next person because there is so much estate if you stop. Satan will try to tell you, your choice makes you a non-believer, you are an imposter and hypocritical, don't listen to nonsensical lies.

EDIT: To avoid confusion, these books are not fictionalized, so actual people should believe it.

Source: in my opinion God is a woman! Think about that?

I am a man and my sources are from a woman and God therefore women need one source (God)!

THE END!

PART ONE!

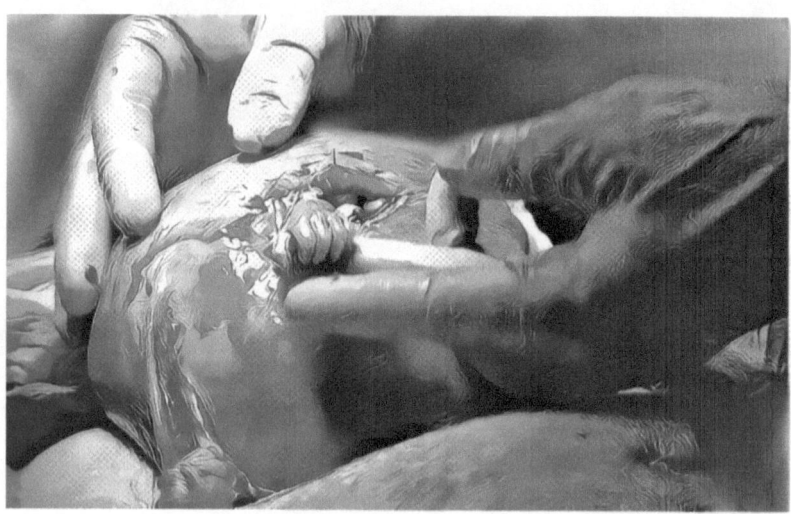

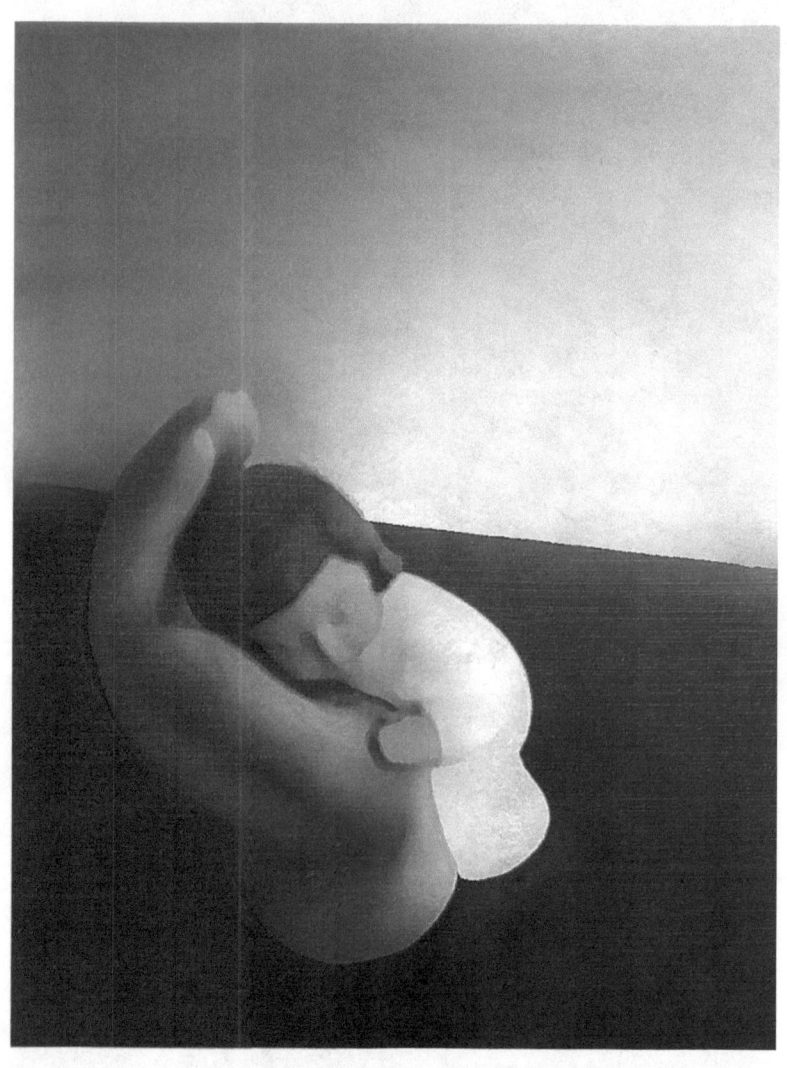

"

My dear readers, you are pro life and that's awesome and that's your choice! Also my dear readers you are in for a treat because 60 percent of the book was written by women and young ladies all over the world. Sharing their experiences or personal stories. I would say you will never read anything like it. With the help of women and young ladies on social media I have gathered enough information to write 5 books. But at some point I had to stop gathering their thoughts and opinions and finish this book, to get the book in your hands. OMG, thank you God.